Writing at Wintergreen

Writing at Wintergreen

An anthology edited by

Helen Humphreys

Wintergreen Studios Press
P.O. Box 75, Yarker, ON, Canada K0K 3N0

Copyright © 2012 by Jennifer Bennett, Sandra Brooks, Helen Coo, Mary Corkery, Diana Claire Douglas, Christine Fischer Guy, Elizabeth Greene, Karen Holmes, Betty-Anne Howard, Lorrie Jorgensen, Danny Lalonde, Ellen McKeough, Lindy Mechefske, Cynthia Mitchell, Amanda O'Donovan, Audrey Ogilvie, Sophie Ogilvie-Hanson, Joyce Sheehey, Nathalie Sorensen, Cheryl Sutherland, & David White. All rights reserved under the International and Pan-American Copyright Conventions. No part of this book may be reproduced in any form or by electronic or mechanical means, including information storage and retrieval systems, without permission in writing from the publisher, except by a reviewer, who may quote brief passages in a review.

Book design by Rena Upitis.
Cover photograph by Faye Ginnies. Photo appearing on page 9 by Diana Douglas; page 69 by Faye Ginnies; pages 51, 52, & 74 by Dawson Hamilton; page 89 by Hayden Rasberry; and pages 5, 22, 29, 30, 55, 56, 62, 72, 80, & 86 by Rena Upitis.

Composed in Book Antiqua and Candara, typefaces designed by Monotype Typography and Gary Munch, respectively.

Library and Archives Canada Cataloguing in Publication
Humphreys, Helen, 1961–

Writing at Wintergreen/Helen Humphreys

EAN-13: 978-0-9865473-8-6

1. Literary Collections—General. 2. Body, Mind, Spirit—General.

I. Title. Writing at Wintergreen
Legal Deposit—Library and Archives Canada

Table of Contents

INTRODUCTION	VII
THE WRITING	IX
MADONNA by JENNIFER BENNETT	1
ALICE by SANDRA BROOKS	2
FOUR DAY LOG by HELEN COO	4
WOODPECKER by MARY CORKERY	7
THERE ONCE WAS A WOMAN TRYING, TRYING TO SIT IN HER CHAIR by DIANA CLAIRE DOUGLAS	9
EXILE by CHRISTINE FISCHER GUY	14
WINTERGREEN RETREAT by ELIZABETH GREENE	20
IN SICKNESS AND IN DROUGHT: OAK TREE REMEMBERING by KAREN HOLMES	23
BREATHE OUT, BREATHE IN, WRITE, OBSERVE, SIT by BETTY-ANNE HOWARD	30
THE 13TH DOCK by LORRIE JORGENSEN	36
HARVEST by DANNY LALONDE	40
STILL, LIFE by ELLEN MCKEOUGH	50

OBSERVATIONS ON RESISTANCE BY LINDY MECHEFSKE	54
ALWAYS NOON BY CYNTHIA MITCHELL	60
PILE OF ROCKS BY AMANDA O'DONOVAN	68
MY CHOSEN PLACE BY AUDREY OGILVIE	71
DRAGONFLY WRITING BY SOPHIE OGILVIE-HANSON	76
NOMENCLATURE OF THE MEADOW FLOWERS BY JOYCE SHEEHEY	78
THE BEHAVIOUR OF TURTLES BY NATHALIE SORENSEN	81
OBSERVATIONS AND REFLECTIONS FROM WINTERGREEN BY CHERYL SUTHERLAND	82
LONG POND ISLAND: A SONG IN THREE PARTS BY DAVID WHITE	89
THE WRITERS	93

Introduction

For three years, for a week in July, I taught a writing workshop at Wintergreen Studios, the purpose of which was to create an original piece of writing inspired by the landscape and environs of Wintergreen. The intrepid workshop participants battled oppressive heat and the more oppressive deerflies, and each chose a spot on the property from and about which to write.

These are the pieces they made during that week in July, three years running. I am proud to be associated with such a fine group of writers, and to have had the privilege of hearing this work when it was created, and reading it again here in the process of compiling this anthology.

The landscape of Wintergreen speaks to all who visit it. The poems and stories in this book are the other side of that conversation.

Helen Humphreys
September 2012

The Writing

Madonna

by Jennifer Bennett

Among the grey ribs of the other dead trees she is not like them,
as though Moore or Michelangelo had
a sculptural rebirth in the brown pond
and then sat too long in a place like this, where
gravity pushes me hard against the granite
and a croaking frog's yellow neck pulses above the mud.

She is the scarred tissue of sun and water become
someone a traveller could stumble toward.

She is a ship's mast broken for lost sailors.
She knows what it is to weep for dead sons
and to hold the infants of daughters.

In a gallery, she stands naked among the clothed paintings.
Children peer into her knot holes, their fingers
searching for fairy tales. Young women hide
their engagement rings in the furrows that rise from
the water marks at her base.
In a cathedral, she hears
the sick old man whisper a prayer for
his wife. Hunched nuns who change the burned out candles
stroke the places where her branches used to be.
She is never lost. She never longs for anything.

This is what perfection is, shattered against the sky,
a space in the air filled with ruin
where the dead are still too strong to fall.

Alice

by Sandra Brooks

Alice got tired of watching her sister play by the river, so the story may go
A tardy rabbit provided an opportunity for an adventure...

Tired of the Kamikaze deer flies on the trail
Thoughts of adventure stray to revenge
I'm hoping every Deet-filled bite brings such a bad taste
I'll be remembered for generations of deer flies to come
Somewhere my karmic wheel rolls backward

Rabbit leads Alice down a hole and the trail leads to a house –
prepared mistakenly for Hobbits.

A house in the woods with grass on the roof
I take comfort seeing the sky is exactly where it should be
There is nothing I would not eat or drink to fit into this
tiny house in the middle of the wild.
Is it considered breaking and entering if the door does
not have a lock?

Alice travels Wonderland
Has a tea party, meets a caterpillar and moves forward
Riddles of a Cheshire Cat guiding her way...

For days I have sat in this house
Put my eyes against each coloured bottle
Hoping there might be answers to my questions that
I swear live on the other side of these looking glasses
The woodstove looks too small to burn witches
My mind panics that I may not have anything
to say at all

Alice becomes BIG then SMALL then BIG again...

My fingers trace smooth marbles and bumpy seashells
My ears strain to hear the ticking of the pocket watch
Stopped at 7:35:58 — does Rabbit knows his watch is here?
A million reflections of me fractured across the slivers of encased mirror
Since no one is looking I make faces
Laughing at my own foolishness until I pull away — not ready to look that hard at myself

Some cards lose their heads, some play chess and before the Queen of Hearts can catch her
Alice awakens to stark reality...

Rooftop grasses entwine themselves around my toes
Without a doubt the view from up here is wondrous
Somehow I feel less vulnerable than when I was curled up napping on pillows
that were courting the favours of sunbeams
For a brief moment I can forget that I have to leave this space that has heard all of my confessions
Like Alice, I too will wake from a dream of rabbits and houses…

Four Day Log

by Helen Coo

Monday

Walk down the road about eight minutes, and look to the left. Do you see the log that resembles an alligator, or possibly a giant squid? Its jaws are open, and it rests motionless in a sea of dead leaves. The chipmunk on the alligator/giant squid's back seems oblivious to the danger. Stupid chipmunk. But maybe puny neocortexes give chipmunks an advantage over humans: their fears are rational, unlike ours.

Tuesday

The alligator/giant squid looks weary. It's decaying on this forest floor, far from the water that sustains it. Moss coats its body, and ants swim over it. Something, a crow probably—why do black atonal birds get blamed for everything while songbirds are held up as angels, even as they scheme to steal others' eggs and nests and mates?—has plucked out the alligator/giant squid's left eye.

How did it get here? I've asked it several times but it hasn't responded. Is it just fashionably late in evolutionary time, perhaps not realizing that the first sea creature made the transition to land millenia ago and therefore it's no longer in a position to change the course of prehistory? Or was it convicted of some heinous aquatic crime and sentenced to exile by a jury of twelve angry alligators/giant squids? Or is it fleeing the maritime equivalent of a Mennonite community—maybe it wants to write a book about its experiences and that's why it refuses to talk? Or is it hoping to achieve the glory of those European explorers of yore, who introduced the potato to the Old World while, to avoid a trade imbalance, exporting smallpox to the new one?

Wednesday

The alligator/giant squid doesn't look any happier today, even though it's more in its element now, waterlogged, its previously grey snout dyed mahogany. Perhaps it is glum, in spite of its fresh new look, at the thought of the time and expense required to maintain a youthful appearance.

Thursday

You may have been wrong, Chipmunk, not to have been afraid of the alligator/giant squid. You're cute, but so was Bambi, who, while walking through this same forest, was gunned down in a hail of bullets usually reserved for the likes of Bonnie and Clyde. Bambi was just a field rat in this neck of the woods. I think the alligator/giant squid may have eaten you after all. It's lolling there in the same satisfied stupor that overcomes all those who have dined well.

It's my last day here, Alligator/Giant Squid, and I'm going to move you to the other side of the road. Slow-moving creatures like you—you've barely progressed an inch since I started watching you four days ago—are likely to get run over by an SUV or, what's more likely on this road, a Toyota Prius.

Oops, sorry, the move did not go smoothly. I dislocated your jaw and part of your skull disintegrated. Forgive my bluntness, but you're no longer an alligator/giant squid; you're just another rotten log. Time for a new story.

Woodpecker

by Mary Corkery

I drag a wrought-iron chair over and plant myself
in the garden, watching a rush of wind heave
bordering maples into green swells.

Maple silvers over our heads on the lawn where I first
befriended insects, before they had names,
when we lived together, the insects and me
and my Dad wearing grey suspenders,
stretched out beside me, propped on his elbow
watching. But what is missing
in that snapshot memory? Where for instance
is my mother?

I see what I saw
then, in our garden by the grey stucco house,
my father who grew food we ate,
huge, magical, attentive father until
I found my way up the hill, onto the highway
toward the world.
My father waves and dissolves in tears,
but I can't see,
my mother.

Here cosmos feather my knee
for attention, taking me to her last autumn (winter
breathing down our necks) when I wrestled
her wheelchair around a lake. Her sudden gasp,
      her hand reaching out to touch
wild pink and mauve cosmos
swaying their hips in a breeze.
    Always loved them, she nods and smiles,
but in vases they die. Her sigh,
Can't be tamed!

We were writing our last chapter,
then   page by page
by word
               touch   voice
                    silence
and then
      mother suspended in thinning air
            beyond the valley, beyond father hoeing,
            beyond me swaying my hips,
                  mother flows away.

Somewhere a woodpecker
     knocks   and knocks
not knowing
     the door is open.

There Once Was a Woman Trying, Trying to Sit in her Chair... [1]

by Diana Claire Douglas

At Wintergreen, I stayed in a small hand-built building called the Meadow Hut which I called my Hobbit House. It was situated a short walk from the main house, following the car tracks through long grasses and wild berry bushes and then dipping down into the woods, a cordwood structure with a curved living roof of spiky grasses. Outside the front door there was a platform and I placed my camping chair on the platform, under the trees.

Once upon a time, as in now, there is a woman sitting in her half-sized camp chair underneath a frilly-leafed canopy made by skinny trees, and she is waiting, waiting for we know not what, but she is waiting, observing what is close by her, using her senses—you know, the five basic senses that everyone uses when they are told to be observant—sight, sound, smell, touch, taste, but the only thing is she is actually a bit handicapped sensorily in this endeavour since she has no sense of smell, not since her first-born son was newly here— shitting and peeing and vomiting as new babes do, and it is since then she stopped smelling although she is not sure if this was by choice or by

---

[1] The tone is thanks to Susan Griffin: "There once was a woman trying to be a writer..." a piece about being a mother and a writer that I read in the mid-80s, and it has stayed with me.

circumstance and now that she is deaf in one ear her slight handicaps are growing so that she is quite dependent on her eyes forgetting she could reach and touch the skinny trees, the carpet of dead leaves, the warmth of the sun on the back of her neck, yes she could touch if only she would remember, but we can see she is concerned about carrying out the exercise, a writing exercise, one you can use to write portions of your novel although she does not think this is a possibility for her, neither using it for her novel or actually finishing this exercise because it's almost impossible for her to sit in a chair and stay there without giving into the desire to get up and move—move anywhere but preferably on this hot, sunny, gorgeous summer day where there is only the slightest of breezes and the trees are silent with each other, not announcing a coming storm with leaves upturned and branches swaying, not even playing with the air and each other in a syncronized dance of joy that the day is THIS day and life is good and full and perfect, no the trees are silent—[or she is also willing to admit she can't understand how they communicate in their silence] on this hot summer's day so she would like to go for a long, slow swim in the pond that is at least 20 minutes away, despite the demonstration of purposeful walking, showing it could be done—it being the walk up and down hills, through trees and bush and branches and rocks jutting out and poison ivy lurking—it can be done in 12 minutes purposefully, but she knows she is not that kind of physically-young anymore and will take at least the full 20 minutes if she were to go walking now, but then again, she feels in this moment she'd rather lie down on her bed and allow the sleepiness that is overcoming her, you know, the head-nodding, eyes drooping, pen-dropping sleepiness that means her 3:15 a.m. wake up is now catching up with her and if, just if she could put her head on that pillow on the lovely bed in her Hobbit Hut, the hut with the low wooden door she must remember to always duck before entering, the hut made of wooden ends and cement and she is sure there is a name for this type of construction but can't remember it now or more likely she's never known the name, but if she could just lie down on that bed she wouldn't so mind the ants who have moved into her hut since she arrived, the busy little buggers chomping their way through the window sill leaving a sawdust pile an inch high in just a day, she wouldn't mind those ants even crawling over her and tickling her bare arms with their tiny little ant legs because they are so much easier to take than the buzzing of mosquitoes and deerflies, now landing on her head, arms, bare feet and sometimes nipping her, sometimes flying away, just as she is about to have the yummy satisfaction of slapping them dead, squished flat, the mosquitoes releasing the blood, her blood, mind you, they have sucked out of her, so she now has a red mark on her skin, a sign of a battle scar, a sign of victory, woman defeats mosquito, although it's a wonder she doesn't have bruises because she has had little success on this afternoon as she sits in her chair waiting for her clock which she brought with her to show her that the necessary minutes have passed but believe it or not the clock has only ticked away 25 minutes and she has 35 minutes to go and she really wonders if she can keep this up, sitting, looking, observing since she wants to be an Alice Walker kind of writer, the kind that just lets the words write through her though she hopes Alice won't be offended since Alice probably observes too but she has always loved the story of the writing of *The Color Purple* where Alice moved across the US four times before the characters were happy enough with her location to tell her their story, so you see she'd rather be this kind of writer than the Maeve Binchey kind who watches and listens to everything around her, even eavesdropping on conversations on the bus and getting off the bus with the talkers so she can hear the end of their conversation to be used somewhere and sometime in a story and she is sure this is a good way to write but she finds it so difficult to not be in her own world, the world she has constructed within her or maybe it is ever-constructing itself within her and she likes to watch the shifts and changes and excitement when a new idea pops in surprising her and leading her on a merry romp but she's always been told she lives way too much in her head and she has to get into her heart, why she wonders, her head being such an interesting place to be, not boring, not at all boring which was a promise she made to herself at age 10, a promise never to be boring, and such a promise, even if it seems an odd one for a 10-year-old, means life is quite an adventure, a multi-dimensional adventure with a multitude of experiences that she can't tell anyone because she knows 1. they won't believe they are true, 2. they will see her as crazy and 3. they are embarrassed by her outrageousness, yes, even though she doesn't say much now, there was a time when she was quite outrageous and just said what she wanted to say without thinking of the complications to her life and sometimes to her very soul this kind of free expression caused so now she has learned to say little and write a lot to herself, write not for public consumption but because she must let someone know, even if it is just the white pages with blue lines of her journal she must tell someone and she does this as

she waits for her characters to arrive to tell her what they want and why they want it and who they need to have with them in their story, which she has promised she will faithfully record word-for-word, if only, if only they would come to her soon, like now, yes she prays, please come soon.

Exile

by Christine Fischer Guy

We pace and curse and tell lewd jokes. Owing to the lack of space and relative poverty of our surroundings, it is not always possible to recreate the heady days at the academy, but so far we have been unwilling to give up on the idea. We might have been delivered here against our will but we can make of this place what we wish. We expect no visitors.

We knew everything. We were hypotheses and stratagems and theories. We proved and disproved, taking equal pleasure from each. We expounded and lectured and published, never once thinking that what we had might be temporary. The spider hurries along the windowsill, chances the pane, then rests at the opposite edge, thinking of webs. We were like that once.

We were sitting on the steps outside the main academy building, passing a pipe filled with aromatic herbs, discussing the beginning of the world. We had hit upon 'goddamn particle' to describe the place of lack in our current theory. It was only an expression of frustration, no disrespect to the regime's religion intended. The theory was developing in the usual way, the result of hours of argument and competitive postulating. We were loud, but this was not unusual. The police would remind us to keep our voices lower if we lost track of our own volume.

But there was no warning. No siren wailed, no club was raised in signal. When the military bus pulled up, our conversation slowed only briefly and then resumed. We felt no threat. We were close, it seemed, to a resolution. We felt we'd almost cracked it. Then we were surrounded and everything went black.

Judging by the lumps on our heads, we concluded that clubs, not drugs, had been the cause of our new situation, packed into the small bus, facing each other, knees pushed together. And still we were not panicked; nothing in our lives to that point had lead us to fear. The new regime continued to tend the buildings and gardens at the university.

Our captors said nothing until we reached the edge of the sea. There was to be no trial, the big one told us, as though reading our thoughts. Our blasphemy, coupled with the incontrovertible proof of our writings, made us not only unwelcome inhabitants of the new city, but unnecessary ones. We made only ideas, he said, and what worth were these on the open market? What product would these contribute to the new economy? We had overstepped boundaries we hadn't known existed. We would have argued, protested, tried to persuade, but our tongues were stopped with rags. Alcaeus slipped his elegant fingers out of their ropes and had begun to untie the knot at the back of his head when he was clubbed again.

The raft was leaky on one side. We stayed on the other so it would admit only a little sea water and watched the shore recede. It was a surprise how swiftly the current carried us out to sea. The sun beat on our bare heads and shoulders without mercy and eventually we were forced to use our heavy winter cloaks, the only extra piece of clothing we were given. The heat under them was stifling. Pindar, never of a stout constitution, swooned twice. We revived him with handfuls of sea water just cool enough to startle his hot skin. We didn't dare use the fresh water they gave us, only five wineskins full: one for each and one to spare. The wine itself we also saved, knowing we would want it when night fell.

Time passes in this little hut we built ourselves. Only our longer hair and beards confirm this as truth. Dragonflies seem a trick of light with their aimless yet urgent flight. A small creature is burrowing, chewing a spiral path from one end to the other of an overhead beam, hewn with rough strokes by our single axe. We were clumsy with the hand work, removed from our abstract familiars. We slept under the stars for the seven nights until it was finished, slumping into sleep around a fire pit we'd dug with our hands after arguments fueled by too much wine. Only Horace was useful with any instrument but a pen. We were thankful that his father had tried, unsuccessfully in the end, to teach his son a trade, but Horace knew enough of wood and clay to coax this little shelter into existence.

Alcaeus refused to lift a manicured finger, convinced that a boat would appear on the horizon to take us home. We countered with the obvious facts of our exile—the raft, the wineskins, the axe, for the regime was blinkered but not inhuman—and still he would not help. When the wine was gone, only days after our arrival, he sat with his back to us, watching for any shift in the horizon.

The hut is smaller than it should be, each of us incapable of truly understanding how unsuited we were to close quarters. It was meant to be temporary, until—what? Alcaeus was proven right? We would miraculously find the strength of will to make another, and another, and another? We would die off, or attempt to leave the island? Our lack of foresight humbles us.

We no longer know what we are. We have not spoken of the goddamn particle since that day. We see only slivers of our skin reflected in the broken shards of mirror we found on the beach and Pindar insisted on embedding in the clay wall along with a starfish. We gathered sea shells and lined the ceiling with them. We did not stop until every last inch was ribbed.

Winter is coming on, driving us indoors for longer stretches of the day. Alcaeus continues to wait for rescue, eating only when we offer some of the rabbit or fish we manage to snare, never hunting for himself or any of us. Horace has become ill-tempered about him and brings up the possibility of a second exile, this time from the hut he did not help build. Four of us cover the floor when we sleep, with less room between us than we'd have in a prostitute's bed. With Alcaeus gone, Horace says, we three would find more comfort, have more food in our bellies, and better quench our thirst.

We notice the chink between wall and door almost simultaneously. It will need patching before the snow comes on. With summer gone it will be difficult to prise more clay from the ground at the opposite end of the island, found one day after a heavy rain when we prowled with our emptied wineskins, hoping for puddles deep enough for our purposes. Alcaeus came with us that time. He had joined none of our efforts before that. Water-seeking is his only contribution to this strange new community. His only plan is rescue. We worry about his persistence with this delusion; he had not shown signs of helplessness or dependency in any of our previous dealings with him. Whenever we took meals together at home he was indistinguishable from the rest of us in appetite, if not in stature.

He has grown thinner still. The same is true of all of us, though we three who hunt have fared slightly better. The exercise and the meat make us lean but strong. Alcaeus eats only when we are successful in persuading him to eat a morsel or two. Horace believes that he does not intend to live.

Let him go, he says, after Alcaeus takes up his daily post at the edge of the sea and we have gone hunting. If he does not wish to live, we are wasting our food. By the time the snow comes, we will need to have dried some to make it through the winter. We look up, thinking of the spectacle of meat drying above our sleeping heads. We have not eaten such things before now but we have already begun experimenting with evaporated sea water for salt. We will need it soon.

The hare will stay, Pindar says. There will be other creatures to hunt in winter. Can you so easily forget the way he defended your cataclysm theory of creation? The rest of the academy was against you. Even us.

We know it's true. It was the most contentious of Horace's ideas and it made some furious. Except for Alcaeus, none of us tried to defend him. We might have said that we feared retribution, but in truth we'd thought him wrong. We have since been persuaded. It was a direct route from there to the particle theory.

All of the leaves have gone. The oak sapling just outside our low door is a sad stick in the ground. We have gathered the fallen leaves as bedding. Pindar believes they will bring warmth in the winter. Horace worries about fire. We will be forced to light one indoors soon. Horace knew enough to make a small hole in the roof for this eventuality but it will be smoky in here all the same, and we will be forced into even smaller sleeping spaces. We think of our quarters at the academy, the high ceilings and enormous hearthstones where we might have laid our four heads in comfort and kept warm by the fire.

> All the more reason to let Alcaeus remain, I say. For the extra body heat, the extra cloak.
>
> I might have known that you'd be the one to want to keep him, Horace says. A woman is prone to a kind heart.
>
> Sappho is right, Pindar says. At the very least, he will help keep us warm.

We have been reduced to the sum of our seething cells. The haunting cry of a raptor echoes nearby. We are suddenly alert, searching the sky for our competition.[1]

---

[1] The tiny, perfect 'Hobbit House' lies a kilometer or so from Paddy's Lake on Wintergreen Studios' 204 acres, remote enough from the main lodge to inspire this story. I wrote it in the afternoons, protected from the July heat and deerflies by its live roof and cool walls. The little table overlooked sun-bleached long grass and visiting Great Crested Flycatchers, who took dry baths in the pine needles. Behind me on the stone floor was a small potbelly stove; there were provisions and tin plates and an alcove bed that let me dream awhile. Embedded in the wall with slices of cedar, end-to-end coloured bottles drew jeweled daylight inside.

Wintergreen Retreat

by Elizabeth Greene

I: First View

The first view feels like forever.
This tapestry of wildflowers,
blue, white, green, yellow, pink —
green leaves, flowers
blowing in the wind.
The range of trees beyond
promising wildness, green mystery.

II: The Heat

So intense I peel off
my watch, my shoes, my rings.
If I stayed longer
I'd be stripped to buff,
living in the lake,
all pores and skin.

III: The Bugs

Divebomb our heads
like commandoes out of Star Wars,
turn the great chain of being upside down.
What are brains
to sting and instinct?

IV: The Trees

Like the bugs, here before us,
they make family seem easy —
drop a seed, and when it sprouts,
croon and encourage
in mesmerizing tree language —
feed it on shed leaves
till it grows tall, takes its place
in the community of trees.

V: The Wildflowers

Shapes and names emerge.
Vipers bugloss, blue as a perfect shirt,
purple vetch, white sprays of silverthreads,
mullein, tall green watchtowers,
foxgloves' gangly cousins.
Clover, pink and white, scenting
hot, longed-for breeze.

VI: The Sky

Light blue, stretching to the edge of sight,
butterflies veering crazily, living the truth of
inebriate of air.
Clouds rolling or wispy.
None of them
Bringing rain.

VII: Last Morning

The sun floods the grass gold.
Vetch, daisies, clover old friends now
but new in early light.
The tall mullein have blossomed yellow.

Silverthreads, bloomed into riotous
white chandeliers, are echoed
by the new-blown lilies
in the lesser, planted garden.

In Sickness And In Drought: Oak Tree Remembering

by Karen Holmes

You, you who are there all day,
you who say you want to know what I need:
you and your kind who've forgotten —
who could not say who I was;
I, who have stood here
year upon year,
never changing;
you are but my you.
And yet it is only by tilting your head back
(way back)
that you see them:
the nine-pointed leaves
that you squeezed between bibles
in your bedroom;
brown and brittle, you counted
their corners
pressing your hands upon them,
sitting on your Sunday chairs.
You, now
I feel your weight upon me —
a blue cloudless sky
(smothering in its clarity)
bears down.
And things become desert.
There is a pain there:
amid the fevered landscape,
I hear your secret weeping.
My breath catches:
I tighten, I constrict,

I lift away all those inner tides
of hatred and pity
that threaten to drown you
as you recognize such dryness
as your own creation.
        It has all become much more difficult.

How could you not know these things?
I am not so different.
I have also worked here.
I too have lifted rock and stone,
I too have cut through the tangle of roots
and stirred up swamp grasses;
all to make earth —
black and hidden —
out of pine needles, twigs and leaves.
My roots burrow down
to build homes:
holes for voles and
chipmunks returning with their jowled loads;
microbes and maggots,
death's devourers.
I am young yet.
Not so long ago, I travelled out,
eager to hear your voices
in wet circuitous groves,
in crafted stone circles,
and round jungle temples and oracles.
Nemetons to Diana. Fessas.
Apollo. Brighid.
Adjidaumo and Netimus.
All the names you have forgotten.
There, gathered rain from my branches,
poured onto bellies —
incantations for babies and magic:
The Hard-Tree, the Power-Tree,

the Strength-Tree, the Semen-Tree.
I remember the words of the ancient earth-speakers.
    That cord has been broken.

I stay in place now,
living my matter to maximum.
Lichen eyes
inch out of rock,
silently watch me.
I know they are alive:
at night I hear a slow heavy pulse
echo out from their crystal centres.

I can exist here
for quite some time, you know:
just a bit of water to drink
and a few snatches of gestured conversation
between bobbing ferns
and waving seedling trees
in this my forest-nursery.

And I am not unhappy in my work:
above, the desire of stars;
below, the memory of all trees —
my rivers of bark between
antennae of water, earth, and air.
Memories ascend to the stars,
visions return to my roots:
These stories I tell
in gentle tones of leaf-muffled breezes.

My world is green — green and yellow —
The colours of a child's bedroom:
A bird at the window,
the white curtains — rising, wringing,
buzzing life —

lift and ripple their arms
into the centre of the houses
I have built for you.

      I have seen your children here:
acorn cups for dollies' parties,
sticks for swords
and some chambered hearts of walnuts shells
to hang as pendants round little necks,
gifts for mother.
And I have heard you tell them to be careful;
the scripts set,
the rules enumerated,
the interdictions given
to stay between the nuisance-stones
you'd hauled off fields,
dumping here as boundary.
      (You do not ask them what they're doing.)

Mothers scream, red-faced, large,
bolting from clean kitchens
desperate for order,
hair pulled tight across temples
(their white churches the place to be
scoured and sanctified);
fugitives from an immovable She
expecting the work done by tomorrow.
      Farmers, too resentful to be fathers,
short with dark skin of thick leather,
ragged side burns, faces barely shaven,
big dogs and felt hats,
hauling and sweating and lying;
their unending labour a shield from liquor
(a chain for the heart):
and these rock altars an homage to their
chosen enemies:

the wives, wolves, and neighbours;
coyotes, shades and foxes.

Sometimes I could hear you singing
and you would join us in our living:
memories of wooden lunch pails and
rounded pats of butter;
ginger beer
and boiled eggs pressed between thick slices
of brown crusted bread;
barrels of oak strips — wet and shrunken
against rings of iron, brass and metal;
funeral caskets laid
in our earth we were making;
a wooden horse between small hands
folded upon the chest;
the brief sweet odour of our communion.

But then the repeated misunderstandings,
the same angry words
shouting down any threat of intimacy;
living No, taking Yes:
the constant work;
the barrage of deadlines.
      Later,
blinds pulled,
the standard lamp turned up to its
brightest setting (whether in June
or in January);
the skim milk blue and shivering;
breakfast, lunch and dinner
in the refrigerator.

And then the silence:
only the sound of the lichens' boring
the birds creaking,

the flies buzzing in their endless generation,
and what I could do with this
small dominion you gave me.
                Latest,
                  you have come here:
to build again with soft lumber and machines
a new kind of country;
and your strange rare flowers,
with the names of goosenecks and lilies,
stand specimen amid stones against the wall,
beckoning green-backed hummingbirds
and buzzing bees —
singers of the ancient songs.
                      Once again I hear them.

If you, dearest you,
ask me what I want,
I will tell you:
I want to hear the water.
I need to hear your water.
Sweet water this,
it must bubble through
all that is
to become what we are now
in this your writing.
The woman's voice
must no longer be
muffled through slabs of thick butter,
bread and heavy laundry.
Allow the rings about your heart to open,
arc out and into me.

A white wolf stood here once,
two hundred summers ago
Jupiter lay next to the Sun.
This sweet smell of you,

this summer light
conjures her here before me.
Listen. Listen. Listen.
She touched me with one padded paw,
and I have not forgotten.

Breathe Out, Breathe In, Write, Observe, Sit

by Betty-Anne Howard

Day One:

Colours pink on the hollyhocks, they open, they close,
rarely in that order. They are tall & lanky.
How can there be two pinks on the same branch?
Dark, light, no two alike — flowers that is, like people. The
bee hovers over the leaf looking for a flower.
Or is she just resting?

At a distance I see the forest. Why do colours bring tears
to my eyes? How many variations of green are there, how
many different types of trees? What was it like for our
ancestors to go trudging through the forests looking for a
place to build a home?
It would have nothing to do with the view.
Or would it?
Weren't they all the same?
Did they pick out the biggest trees for thick walls, or
smaller ones, easier to fell?

The burgundy has
turned to red, that's
what the sunlight
did to it,
intentionally
but not purposefully
How did the
hollyhocks become
so fascinating, how
did that happen?

The better question for me is how did they manage to not let the bugs bite them, tear them to shreds? That's why I gave up on hollyhocks. I left them to the bugs, it was either that or poison them — the bugs that is.
And that destroyed the plants too.
Can't have your cake & eat it too.

I hear the bugs, there's one in particular that keeps hurling itself against the window.
What the hell is his problem, what exactly is he trying to prove?

Why can't all the spaces between the rocks, where the pebbles lie, have little pink flowers?
Actually they are purple, how can you see purple & write pink?

How can plants grow from stone? A question that once perplexed me. I tied it to being poor — how would I know that plants needed soil, my parents were too busy not taking care of us to take care of plants too. I knew how the world worked. I understood it better than most. I just didn't know how to put words to it — or maybe I was just afraid that the words I knew weren't your words and I didn't believe mine were the right ones, so where does that leave you?

Without a voice or one that is a mirror for yours?

Sometimes you see the yellow in the middle of the purple pansy; it helps when they are being framed by the yellow wildflowers. Straight ahead it's weeds, or so it seems, across the narrow field there are trees, their branches still, sometimes they lift up as if to wave, as children do when they are first leaving.

I see the dead tree off to my left. I used to see dead trees as free heat, firewood … is it accessible, how easy will it be to get the truck close enough for loading & hauling it home? My gold mine, dead trees.

How do they decide who is going where & in what order? Is there a Master Plan? Does the hickory really care for the maple or would she prefer to be next to the birch?

I don't see any birch here. It's clouded over, the breeze is making the trees shimmer. The bugs have a harder time landing, on me especially. You don't notice the dead ones at first, as your eye is drawn to the beauty of the plant, but then you see them, all scraggly & brown.
Done in, they've had their time in the sun, they've bloomed the sun devoured them & they have nothing left to give.

Except their seeds of course, which if plucked too soon won't give you their seeds. So, they're teaching you patience.
If it's seeds you're after, you could save some $, just like the dead tree.

But you have to be able to see the world that way. Patience is the key.

What if you chopped down the tree & it wasn't dead? You would have to wait even longer to use it, to heat your home, so why would you do that? Chop it down when there's plenty of dead ones around, you just have to go looking & then ask.

How many times have you gone into a situation in life when it's had win-win written all over it, only to find out it wasn't a dead tree, after all.

Day Two:

Eagle or turkey vulture flying, in the sky, wings folding, opening, disappearing behind the trees, grasshopper standing still, on a branch, wondering where to go next or stay put. Beady-eyed dragonfly gets tired of flapping.

I see the lavender through the branches that open in my view with a peach petal flower in its foreground. White pink yellow pink, all very colorful in my view, with my legs outstretched absorbing the sun's rays,
feeling the heat burn my skin.

I keep my legs in front of me, on a chair, not crossed below me,
so I can see the little bastards before they bite me & kill them, yes kill them, the little bastards.
They seem less interested in legs above the table — rather than below. Death awaits them, if they only knew.

Pacing was one of the topics this morning, my pace has really slowed, while my agitation has grown.
How can that be when all I have to do is observe, record, observe. Breathe in, breathe out — relax into it. Feel my tummy expanding.

I want a cloud, won't one come up, just for me, a gift from god, just what I asked for.

Meanwhile, my ass is sore from sitting. I fidget, I feel hot all over, my skin is no longer burning in the spots touched by the sun because I've drawn my legs up into me. Now the heat wave is happening all over me, the sweat in my arm pits bubbles up. I want to see something. My body sighs, a deer, a bear, shouldn't something be running across the field?

Day Three:

Sitting still, sitting very still, breathe in, breathe out, meditate if you have to, do what needs to be done because you have one hour to do it in.

Sometimes I wish I could automatically be transported, through the portal where Catherine's words would be sitting there waiting for me, to be affixed to my story, making it sound attractive & publishable.

Helen's encouragement is flowing over, like a waterfall whose reservoir keeps filling up as quickly as it spills over. And once through that portal Helen's eyes light up with each written word, yes, yes, keep it coming, engaging in a sexual act that is neither.

Cynthia is there dispensing her sage advice about how to remain free, inside a marriage, which is what will happen the next time around, given the opportunity. And really, when it comes right down to it, none of this matters because her flapping arms will mean, sooner or later, she'll take flight. The view from there will be so enticing she won't want to land, ever again.
I mean would you, after all that taking off effort?
I don't think so.

Your lover this beautiful breeze, making the flying a lot more interesting — more blue than grey to enhance the beauty of your sky.

As I sit, the sun on my legs, yet again, before starting to sweat & then needing to remove them, from the sun, but I hold them out, like meat on a BBQ, without the turning. That could only be done if I were lying on my tummy & then writing would be difficult — not that it isn't difficult now.

My hand is hurting from all this writing, I'm not complaining though. What I really want to know; is this a test, & in the end, will I be the most embarrassed because I didn't do it right & everyone else did? My sad sack ofwriting will be left out, intentionally, purposefully. Little meat on her bones, like her writing. No one would believe what's below the surface, at least with water you can see what's there — provided it's clear enough.

As a kid you can't possibly know what's below the surface. I tried making mine small, clean, smooth as possible. You had a choice, you could either slip off easily & quickly so you never really noticed much or remained clean so there was never any smell that would linger or be associated with you. Being poor was dirty business, a type of stench, unlike shit that could dry & make the smell disappear.

I feel bugs on my skin that I'm not even sure are there but I slap myself anyway, just in case. I drink my water. I am taken away from my writing & still I write. Where did I go?

Come back to me baby, like feeling your touch on my skin, notice the raspberries, even though you can't see the red, until you get up close & there they are.

The 13th Dock[1]

by Lorrie Jorgensen

Buddy waves over to me and yells "hi," his pubic hair and penis a black fuzzy circle in the middle of his groin. Doesn't he know I have a writing assignment to complete? Helen said to start with the emotional heart of the story. Now I'm stuck with Buddy's penis as my enduring image and I don't even like penises. I mean, they're okay but it's not like I want one for myself.

The splash of Buddy diving in the water is echoed by Gracie, jumping off a rock to chase a loon, which has been teasing her for days by fishing close to our dock. She never gets close enough to sniff or circle, and today the loon warbles out sharp cries, and flutters along the surface using its wings, as if to say come chase me, before diving away. It resurfaces next to the green canoe that the Andersons keep tethered to their dock. Gracie reluctantly turns and swims back to me.

Our lake is called Green Lake. It is small and private, its circumference divided by thirteen properties. I've counted them several times, hoping with each tally that I am wrong and there are 12 or 14 instead. I'm not a superstitious person but I'm tempted to erase one of the docks that line the lake, but like the image of Buddy, it's difficult. But it should be hard, shouldn't it? It shouldn't

---

[1] Lorrie attended the workshop during the day, but went home to the "13th dock" in the evenings, a 15-minute drive from Wintergreen.

be easy to rid yourself of relationships because of a superstitious whim or a wanton careless dismissal.

Who would I pick anyway? Would it be John and Manjit and their two beautiful blonde-haired daughters who come by kayak, and walk shyly up the steps holding hands, to give me the lake newsletter every year? Or should I simply erase Audrey and Dave and their slew of boys, Dylan, Devin, Dixon and Dave Jr., because the young ones are screamers and the older boys are loud and obnoxious, especially when throwing each other off the dock or arguing about what movie to watch when it's raining?

Buddy is swimming out to the middle of the lake and I follow his line to consider other docks. How about the buyers of the Sellers cottage who rent it out? Once to an asshole that launched a seadoo and drove it around and around Snake Island for a half hour, a return trip of no more than a minute. Should I blame them and erase their dock as fast as the seadoo guy left when he realized people had come down to the lake and were on the end of their docks yelling at him to go away?

Rosemary and Peter didn't yell of course. Peter canoed over and I imagine him explaining to the seadoo man, in his quiet understated manner, that the lake was a no motor lake and if he could please take his machine out of the water. He probably asked him if he needed help with getting it back on its trailer. Peter also checks the clarity and quality of the water and Rosemary e-mails a list of all the birds that have visited the area, bi-annually. Like with penises I'm not a bird person either, but the idea of erasing their dock just doesn't seem right. It would be an abomination.

I could choose Frank. He's single and owns the least amount of shoreline. In this case, less is not more. He could go. But I like Frank and he lets me gather firewood from his property and I take care of Annie, his black lab, when he's away. I can't have a fifth dog, so Frank stays.

Rich and Annette don't like dogs but house two cats. I could toss them. It would be difficult because I admire their preciseness and sense of detail. The writing on the carriage bolts used to fasten the corners of their dock all line up straight and level to the swimmer who reads. The joints are tight, with impossibly equal spaces between the boards, whose ends and edges are all sanded to a quarter inch radius. Who does that? I know who.

I look at my own weathered and beaten dock. It's a pressure treated frame topped with red cedar that has now turned a soft grey. One board is lifting at its end where I set the screws too deep, creating a well for water that has gathered and rotted the wood. The patina at its end is scratched and gouged with the nails of dogs leaping into the lake, chasing Kongs and diving bodies. Chairs and dropped bottles have dented and marred the decking and a rusted beer cap has wedged itself between two boards.

What if I'm the 13th dock? I'm sure the never ending drunk crowd of women swimming naked was obnoxious and annoying, at least to some of my neighbours. And though I don't party anymore, I also don't distribute the newsletter or test the water or count the birds, and while my dock is not precise or pristine as others, it is a step above the jumble of walkways, ramps and decking that Buddy and Marilyn have cobbled together. Theirs is a floating marina that shelters a canoe, a catamaran, a rowboat, a windsurfer, a pedal boat, a kayak and a sea kayak. I realize they have too many water toys to blink away quickly and decide the number 13 must be a lucky compassionate number somewhere. I'll need to do some research.

Buddy is climbing back onto the dock, his ass white and bright against the dark tan of his back. It gets brighter and a bit more hairy when he bends over and starts to bail the rowboat. I really should do part of the writing exercise Helen assigned. Observations and whatever else comes from sitting still, swatting flies and sweating in one place for an hour. I look around urgently for something, anything. There, I've got it.

> *I observe that the branches of the white pines that stand on guard across the lake look like rock shelves and I could use the fissures as steps to climb to the crown of the tree where I could gather in the bottom of the clouds pulling their fluffiness into my face like cotton candy at the fair.*

Fuck, that's awful, but I'm out of time.

Harvest

by Danny Lalonde

Brian wants to walk on water. There are many things he wants to do, but Brian thinks that if he starts with the water that everything else will follow easily. So, early one Saturday morning while Beth and the kids are still in the cabin asleep, Brian clambers down the rocky slope to the water and onto the dock that leads into Otter Lake.

Brian slips out of his sandals, and stretches a tentative foot down over the still surface. Something like a prayer runs the length of his concentration and sounds like "*JesusFatherMotherMaryJoseph...*" over and over again. He exercises great faith because the endeavour demands it. Most everything he wants to do requires great faith.

As he leans his weight out toward the leading foot, Brian flexes that part of his psyche that wants to believe in the divine. Slowly, in thoughtful increments, he studies the line of light closing between the water and his flesh. In that small space, he feels the coolness of the lake before touching down.

He teeters a moment, doubting his ability to balance between faith and flesh much longer. The dock, which he has built, is a full foot higher than the water—a flaw in the design. The big muscle in his thigh tightens (the one still planted on the dock) and the fleeting hint of a cramp wants to crawl in there between the sinewy tissues and roll around.

He extends his arms, and carefully, in a motion as delicate as Tai Chi, Brian shifts the rest of his weight off of the dock. Immediately, he finds himself, for a glorious instant, standing one foot in the air, and one foot balancing on the water.

The haze that has dragged the morning in with a pall immediately evaporates, from above him a bird suddenly cries out, and the full light of sunrise throws a glare across the lake so brilliant and immortal that Brian pitches backward onto the dock and nearly knocks his head off against one of the posts supporting the long pier.

Only a moment. Not enough to say "walking" necessarily, but he has been there on that line, carried by his faith. He has been there (*thank you JesusFatherMotherMaryJoseph*) on top of the water. Across the narrow lake, there is a boy struggling to slide a canoe into the water, his thin body as white as bones. Brian watches the boy wave toward him and he wonders if the child has been a witness to this morning's miracle.

If only Beth and the children had been here to see.

I should rebuild the dock, he thinks. It was a mistake to mount it so high. Beth won't let the children out here alone, even with life jackets. What good is a lake without children?

Beth and the kids still haven't come out of the house. Beth often reminds him that it isn't a house. It is only a cabin. But he has insulated it, weather-stripped the doors and windows, installed a larger woodstove than the small pot belly that had been there when they moved in. The only similarity left to a cottage is the screened porch with its small rusty table and solitary lawn chair, the oil lamp hung in the window frame, and there in the corner, a wooden box full of jigsaw puzzles, most with pieces missing. Only the screened porch of the cabin is quaint and seasonal. For him, the rest is as robust as home. For Beth, he thinks, all of this is temporary. It is, in fact, a cabin with acreage, and with land there is always more.

Land is the thing, isn't it? he thinks. *Land defines adulthood, defines ambition, defines success.* Some of the land is brambled and twisted into impossible tangles of wildflowers and bushes, unrecognizable amalgams of trees and wiry shrubs that want to shoot as high as the horizon. Some of the property is cleared, though, and another small meadow was easily ploughed and planted with something like a prayer unrolling in his head: *JesusFatherMotherMaryJoseph.*

When they visit vineyards for research, disguised as tourists, stealing photographs of the plants, snapshots of the fruit and the trellises, Beth is always cautious, sceptical.

> "Nobody grows grapes this far east or this far north," she says.

> "We'll be the first," he assures her, but Beth will not be convinced and would not simply believe.

> "Have faith," he tells her.

> "I'll support you, Brian. Whatever you want to do. I will always support you; you know that."

But it wasn't true. She had stopped being supportive, hadn't she? She was full of doubt, full of questions, full of her injurious adjectives and selfish pronouns. Her support for this adventure falls away too quickly to talk of *her* children and *her* life.

Brian wants to go back to another time. If only he can sustain it, everything else will follow easily. Beth is beside him in the bed and they are young and naked and they can just be here cupped together without lines, without barriers, without those strange lonesome looks they flash each other lately. Their touching bodies tangle, alive in the glory of the moment, undulating in the dance of their excitement. There are no children yet, and her skin is impossible, her mouth wet, and her beauty unfathomable. Holding on to this requires more faith than walking on water.

There is a line, he thinks, like the space between his foot and the water just before he touches down, when anything is possible. *And you have to believe as you cross that line in the unexpected inevitability of all things good and glorious.*

Are they still asleep? he thinks, puzzling a little over their absence this morning.

When the children are babes, one still in diapers, Brian keeps his job in the city and the ordeal of balancing the vineyard is a tiresome commute, is full evenings and unbearable labour through exhausting weekends. Beth tends to the babies, paddles cautiously in the water close to shore, and in waning bursts of encouragement, fills all of them with lemonade and smiles. When the vines are mature enough to bear fruit he quits his job.

Beth faded right away, he thinks. *As though I might outgrow this.*

"A little faith," he tells her. "This will work."

"But your job," she says, discouraged. "What about me and the kids."

"You mean *us*."

"I *mean* me and the kids."

He has been up late working on jigsaw puzzles, meticulously finishing every single one of them, carefully noting the missing pieces from each box with a circle or two marked in pencil on the lid. *If I find the pieces*, he thinks, *I can erase these marks*. Here, there is never the full picture. There is always some detail spoiled by labels, tags, notes, the name of the structure or the artist, something in the way, obstructing the perfect view of the whole image. There is always guessing with puzzles, hoping that the thing will organize itself, become obvious, apparent, or pull itself together.

Here is a puzzle, he thinks, as he hikes back up from the lake, a pair of deerflies tracing a confusion around his head. *When do you know when to move on?* Brian trails across the yard away from the cabin and down toward the field. Here is the barn that Brian built. There is a line crossing the path, a wire, or a shank of thin, thin rope that he does not recognize tracing through the dirt and grass. *Here is a puzzle*. He stops with the toe of his sandal stepping across the cord.

> This time, he speaks out loud. "What is this doing here?"

He looks back up toward the house expecting to see Beth and the children in the bay window smiling, laughing at the lark at having laid this line here for no particular reason except to arouse his attention. The bay window is dark, the cabin a dead hulk across the yard. *They have slept so late*, he think. There is something like a prayer for them he mumbles: *JesusFatherMotherMaryJoseph*, he says inside, and then out loud: "Keep them."

Brian can't remember letting go. He cannot remember when the little changes happened, when he constructed the algebra that has added up to this. He waves away the flies, but they will not be discouraged. There are only the little changes, aren't there? The iterations that repeat, shift, repeat, shift, until you find yourself in a place, as a thing you don't recognize.

He turns toward the field, his foot still stepping on the line in the sparse grass which he feels through the sandal as sharply as a stone. The trellises stretch beyond a rise in wide rows. *Rows of promise*, he thinks. *When the fruit comes*, he thinks, *everything else will follow easily*. Brian lines up Beth and the two children in a gentle row at Christmas and sets the camera to take their picture. He rushes to them to be in the picture with them. Instead, he trips and spills over the Christmas tree knocking everything out of place. What a strange picture the camera takes: all of them are turned away reaching to rescue the tree and Beth looks toward him with supreme, nearly absolute disappointment. He lines them up again to take the right picture, but this one never makes it to a frame. Even the small change retains the dishonesty of the previous moment with Beth's face twisted in despair.

A June bug panics in a too early flight. Brian watches the thing fall from the air and land against a patch of bare ground in front of the barn, its wings like fingernails thrumming aimlessly against the clay casting a huff of dust around it. *I hope I'm not late*, he thinks. Spring seems to have already rolled in full of glory, while he pauses here, stands with his foot on a strange line and the rows of grapevine stretching forever. There is so much to do. There is fertilizer to move from the barn, trellises to patch and vines to pare down. Brian remembers the old tractor and the hydraulic line that burst during the last snow. Brian remembers the tractor parked behind the barn in need of repair.

String is for tying around a finger to remember. String is for holding things together when they want to come apart. Brian moves to the barn and swings the small door wide. This is not much of a barn. *Shed* is too modest a name, but *barn* somehow too ambitious. The tractor was meant to fit inside, but the whole project has come together wrong. There might have been a stall for a horse, or a loft, for climbing up into. He should have built this differently, but the time and the money were never enough. *When the harvest starts paying, then I will build a real barn*, he thinks. *Then Beth will see that this is something real. Then she will see that there is no point in walking away. There are always options*, Brian thinks. *You just need to believe*.

Somewhere in the barn, a chipmunk whistles erratically, insulted by Brian's interruption.

"What do we need all that fertilizer for?" she says.

"For the plants," he says.

"And the diesel?"

"For the tractor."

"It's too much," she says. "Can you afford it?"

"You always say that," he says. "We'll be fine."

Brian struggles suddenly, spinning in the spider web logic of his morning. *Why are they not already awake chasing down to the barn in their rubber boots and dungarees? Has something happened?*

Brian traces the yellow line of cord with his eyes. It snakes behind the cans of diesel and bags of fertilizer.

Has something happened?, he thinks. *Why are they not awake?*

He feels sweat overwhelming his brow and dripping down his face. Brian reaches into his pocket for a rag. He always has a rag. Instead, he opens his fist to a lighter. "I don't smoke," he says.

What have I done? he thinks, trying to remember everything before the miracle. There is something like a prayer thundering in him: *JesusFatherMotherMaryJoseph what have I done?*

Brian flexes that part of his psyche that wants to accept the redemption of the divine but there is something like a cramp sliding in there between the flesh and the faith.

I made a list, he thinks. *Didn't I make a list? I always have a list.*

He digs into the other pocket and pulls out a folded recipe card. He has enough things to do buzzing around his head to fill a notebook: lines of chores and things undone that want for a string tied around a finger. This card is all he can find last night when he sits to plan. There are two things on the list that have already been crossed out. *Blotted* is a better word—worked and reworked with a pencil twisting little circles so that the two lines are unreadable and the card is bruised with the rubbing over it. They are gone and he can't even remember them. The third thing is about the water, and Brian searches his other pockets for a nub of pencil, but there is nothing else in there. Number four is this thing with the lighter. Number five is a number with a tiny period of a dot beside it. He doesn't remember what number five is to be, but he believes that it will come to him as soon as he gets through number four. After he gets through number four, everything else will come easily.

There had been a dream last night, he thinks: *Children laughing between trees, telling me to wake up and come along as though there was something to be missed if I waited*. Brian thinks of the boy across the lake and wonders if he was really waving or beckoning.

Brian closes the barn door and crouches outside by the end of the yellow line traced through the dull grass. The lighter takes three strikes to light, but the cord catches easily and burns with a chasing spark. He feels heat rising in himself, the want to slow things down while somehow being pulled strenuously onward. *How do you know*, he thinks, *when it's time to move on? How does Beth figure out something like that? Here is a puzzle with too many missing pieces; if only I had a pencil to mark them down,* he thinks. Absently, he squeezes the recipe card in his fist. He leans his weight first on one foot and then the other, moving slightly closer toward the barn, and steals another look over his shoulder to the empty bay window to see if anyone is watching. He thinks of the thin bony boy on the lake with his canoe and wonders if he will be a witness. For Brian, there is something like a prayer choking him, yet he cannot speak the words. There is a glorious moment of thunderous silence, and then, just as suddenly, Brian feels himself lifted up, and impossibly filled with light.

Still, Life

by Ellen McKeough

I am at the beginning of the trail to Paddy's Lake, digesting the shame that comes from not having braved an outpost in the woods. I circled the lodge three times before accepting I would go no farther. There are hundreds of acres of wilderness available to me but, like a domesticated animal, I hunker down within running distance of home. Armed with the encumbrances of the tourist — sunscreen, bug spray, a bottle of water, a watch, and a blue-and-white striped towel — I lie down and wait for nature to reveal its mysteries.

Ants look like they are easy to make, just two cinches in a strip of living brown.

I lie on my belly, staring into a clump of grass. If I lift my eyes, I can see a copse of trees. My first thought is: Every shade of green is represented here. But that is just the sort of pap that would occur to a person like me in a situation like this. Every shade of green in the world is not represented here. I am forgetting the trees of the Amazon, the jungles of Asia, and the savannahs of Africa. Never mind the rest of Frontenac County: there are only deciduous trees across from my little nest. In my rush to be overwhelmed, I have forgotten the grey-greens of the undersides of conifers.

There is an ant hauling a dead fly over blades of grass and hillocks of earth, earth which is green, brown, grey all at once.

I am bored by this already. I cannot name any of the plants, so they remain unavailable to me. The only shape I feel confident in is the maple leaf. Immediately I discern what looks like a sprig of hemp. It is more than plausible that someone from the lodge could have consumed something akin to hemp out here. I stick it in my mouth. It has thousands of rough ciliae on its underside, probably to protect it against consumption by insects. There is no smell and none of the expected taste.

The ant is hauling the fly over the expanse of my blue-and-white towel. I flick it away.

My interest shifts to an old maple tree. I am no expert in the age of trees, but it is old. This one is taller than most maples in town. It branches into three main boughs low to the ground. As a child I needed a boost to get into the first crotch of the maple in the front yard. Maybe this is not a maple.

The ant is back. Perhaps I am blocking the entrance to its colony. Now it has started up the waffled sole of my running shoes. It is a monstrous amount of work, going up and down my shoe. I flick it away again.

It begins to rain. I have on a canvas hat, a Tilley, that proud Canadian hat with a lifetime Guarantee: "You can leave it in your will," is one of the company's marketing slogans. Rain pings off the stiff, treated canvas of the brim. At first it feels like there is a machine on my head. Then the pinging is coming from me. I am the machine. The pinging takes up all the space in my ears and I can't hear the softer thud of individual drops on the trees nearby.

Because of the light rain, I get off the ground, go to the lodge, return with a chair. Seated, it becomes obvious that the hemp-shaped leaves belong to a plant that stands a foot high and has a yellow blossom. The blossom has five petals, each petal shaped like a Valentine's Day heart, the pointed ends tucked into the tufted centre. I still do not know its name, but now it is something that could be found in a book.

It appears most of the trees aren't individuals at all, but groupings of trees. Conjoined twins and triplets. Earlier I'd wished for a field guide to North American trees, but it would be of no help. None of these silhouettes would match those in the illustrations.

A horse fly collides with the stiff brim of my hat. A prize fighter, it comes back madder than ever.

The rain has passed off to the east. Strips of heat develop on my feet between the straps of my sandals. I stand, and become aware of the road I have been lying and then sitting on, stretching out ahead of and behind me. The gravel is alive with ants. A good percentage of the world's weight must consist of ants and their carcasses.

I am more than I think I am. I can withstand beginning, middle and end. I have the time now, and for the rest of my life I have the time. I love this. Anywhere, anytime.

Observations on Resistance

by Lindy Mechefske

Someone I once entrusted my heart and soul to told me that I was scripted—that I spoke as though delivering lines in a play, and that I had somehow written her into my script. And that she too was delivering lines that were part of *my* script. When I challenged this, she said, "We all have a script that we play out over and over again."

At first I resisted this idea strenuously and after thinking about it for a while, the next time we met I delivered a heated monologue about *not* having a script, about being spontaneous, about not having time or inclination for such a thing. I gave my supporting evidence—all the words and thoughts I had been so carefully accumulating.

"I'm a wife, a mother, an employee, a friend, a daughter. I have two jobs and endless commitments. Who has time for a script?" I said, going on in a similar vein. "I'm winging it as best as I can."

At the end of this, I realized that not only had I just delivered a script, I'd also played out one of the major scripts of my life—one that involves resistance, then reluctant acceptance, and then compliance—usually full, uncompromising, dutiful compliance.

If only I could get through the stages faster—quit the endless internal dialogue, submit, conform and let go. I could move past all the resistance and simply let possibilities unfold—then who knows where my life might take me? I might be travelling the world solo in a kayak, or working as an editor in Manhattan, or living in a remote Mexican village as a Zapotec Princess. I might be a gypsy. Or I might just figure out what I actually want out of life and do that. Perhaps I'm already there.

Finding my writing place at Wintergreen — the space where every afternoon for the duration of our writing workshop I would sit and simply observe and then write about my observations — has been like that. I picked my bedroom as my special spot because I like to retreat into solitude, but I felt a resistance to the place I had picked and to the whole idea in general. I wanted to spend time in other spaces. I particularly liked the spot chosen by one of the other participants nestled into the quiet, un-used back doorway mostly because of the breeze that interrupted the otherwise stifling July heat wave. I wish I could have picked the lake. I thought the front verandah might have been more logical because of the view. I wanted only to finish chapter sixteen of another project I was working on.

I felt like this was a metaphor for my whole entire life… endless longing for something else, endless restlessness.

But despite my resistance, I went back to my room and observed it each day. First I lay on the bed, resting quietly. Slowly I started penciling words, lines, and phrases into my small green notebook.

"Room not changing much," I wrote and then added, trying ever so slightly:

> accumulation of dead bugs on floor and in windowsill
> bed unmade — not part of my usual script
> glass brick tiles along the ceiling. Soft filtered light.
> Black-Eyed-Susans in garden just beyond have remarkable staying power and
> one more bottle of wine gone.

Outside my window a hummingbird darts past, the wing beat audible in the quiet of the day. And I note that the tomato plants have grown taller since I arrived a few days back.

Mine is the back bedroom along the corridor — the room which faces inward onto the vegetable garden. I look out past tomatoes and herbs and kale. I think my room is the nicest of all. It looks and feels like a cocoon. It has a double bed, with a brass frame, and a sumptuous damask and velvet quilted comforter in rich shades of golds, and purples, and burgundy. Every time I lay across the big brass bed, I think of the Bob Dylan song *Lay Lady Lay*, a song I have not heard for years but which now echoes through my mind daily. I'm suddenly horribly nostalgic for Bob Dylan, who I never liked much in the first place.

There are two pieces of art hanging in the room, one of an old arched stone bridge across a rushing brook. The other is of a walled city, which looks suspiciously like York. Both of them remind me of Yorkshire. It feels like an omen. Yorkshire is my heritage, my history, the geography of my heart, the land I left as a young girl.

The room is painted ochre—a colour which sometimes looks deep tan and sometimes pale yellow depending on the light. My small table is covered with the things I brought with me—my ear plugs, my vitamins which I keep forgetting to take, my thyroxine which keeps me alive, my travel clock, and a large stack of books, now toppling over, including *Wuthering Heights*, *The Literary Travel Writer*, Jan Morris's *The World*, with its tattered, dog-eared pages—sections of prose I have tried to commit to memory and more to the point—to commit to heart.

I have two windows, and at night, because there are no curtains on one of the windows, I have watched the night sky and thought of a friend's son—and his beautiful first words—words which came to him so late in his young life—words one might expect of a poet's son. At four years old he looked out into the night and spoke for the first time ever saying simply and clearly, "dark night and fireflies." I have watched the dark night and fireflies and later the moon and the stars. The moon is waning, two nights ago there was a crescent moon at 3:15 am and last night at the same time, there were only stars.

The noise level in my room changes more than anything else. At times, all I hear is the wind in the backdrop of deciduous trees. Other times it is almost entirely still. Sometimes I can hear birds, but late in the afternoon when I am in my spot, the birds are mostly silent. Quiet in the intense heat of the afternoon. As we head towards dinner, there will be a perceptible shift in noise levels as chairs start to scrape the floor, doors open and shut, taps will run, toilets will flush, voices will rise and subside, and I know we are headed towards congregation. At night I can hear the bugs droning and colliding with the window screen, the crickets chirping and a brief chorus of whippoorwills plaintively calling their own name. This afternoon as we work on our pieces, it is strangely silent everywhere. I retroactively add "strangely silent" to my collection of notes.

Sometimes somebody walks past my window their feet crunching on the gravel. Most recently it was the sole male member of our workshop. He was swatting bugs as he went. This simple gesture, his brushing the flies away from his face, makes me almost insanely happy to be in my chosen place, sitting on my bed, observing and writing. I can hide here, in the heat, naked or in my underwear. Nobody knows. And there are no flies except those laying dead on my floor. Dutifully I add "Danny swatting bugs," to my list.

My list of observations is now a full two pages long though granted my notebook is small. But still, I am surprised by the extent of notes I have made without even really trying.

* * *

Suddenly I notice that there are two paint colours in the room, the exterior walls are painted ochre and the interior walls are painted a soft butter yellow.

It is not the changing light, or the intensity of light, or anything so dramatic or romantic, simply my limited powers of observation that have caused me to think that the room is different colours at different times of the day. The room has been painted this way on purpose. I have been laying on my big brass bed for four days observing my room in silence and I have only just realized this. It is a staggeringly simple observation — a new way of looking at things — the realization that seeing takes time and patience.

I make a final notation in my notebook. "Observation takes time and patience. Sometimes seeing the simplest things takes the keenest observation and makes the most impact." And then I think a little bit more and add, "Resistance is futile." But that is not quite right. I erase the word futile and write instead, "Resistance is complex."

I shut my little green notebook. I let a creeping surge of happiness wash over me. I rewrite my script. I am ready for the next chapter.

Always Noon

by Cynthia Mitchell

To Karen—the Keeper of Mother Earth (It's true you know. A bee told me this morning, literally as I penned the words).

To the Goddess Diana of the Divine Feminine Energy— Together you are the spirit and energy of the word.

And to Betty-Anne—thank you for seeing my light; and you owe me part two of your story!

* * *

At noon today I found my writing place, a tiny little one room cabin with a single bunk loft space. It is furnished with a narrow table that folds out, a cute cylindrical wood stove, a futon, a tiny portable IKEA type kitchen, cute knickknacks, candles, and a lounge chair mattress in the loft.

On the ledge there are six CDs—Grateful Dead "In the Dark" being one of them, Dire Straits, Six Strings North of the Border, Don Alder, James Taylor, and Wag World Acoustic Guitars Volume 1. I don't see a CD player anywhere.

There are also a few volumes of books, but the one I pulled out is a leather bound book called *The Doctor* by Isabel Cameron originally published in 1915. What caught my attention was the "Foreword"...

> In sending forth this nineteenth and enlarged edition of *The Doctor*, the publisher has asked me to write a foreword. "But what shall I say?" I asked in dismay. "Oh anything," he replied easily. "People never read Forewords; they're just put in for the look of the thing."

That made me laugh and since I have been commissioned to find a writing space and record my observations, I thought randomly reading snippets of *The Doctor* would be a good place to start.

The writer went on to say that, "the writing of it [*The Doctor*] has been a sheer labor of love, and if I have managed to capture and convey to the reader, some stray gleams of the winsome personality of the original, then I am content." Little did I realize how deep the truth; that the foreword was written for me, for me the writer.

* * *

At noon today I decided to try my vantage point from the loft space, figuring if I start high I might get some divine intervention to the start of my piece. There is a lovely little window that overlooks the marsh and the lake and you can hear the wind rustling through the trees. Voices of the people down at the lake, the only indication that I am not totally alone; that there is life outside my head.

Beside my little ajar window is a small canvas of purples and blues. An abstract multimedia piece with uplifting expressions: "tranquil full recovery," "or an instant we are weightless," "diaphanous wisps," "clouds draw a path for him to follow," "he toys with my phantoms," "*pour le soulagement temporaire*," "Hercules comes often to the edge of the world," "this languid beauty." And being the Capricorn that I am, I must record them all. It is a pretty little piece.

In the center of the back wall of the loft is a small stained-glass window of a tulip or an angel, depending on your perspective. And since I am up here for divine inspiration, I'm going with the angel.

The chorus from my stomach and the tree seeds making their way along roofline the only chorus from on high I heard in my loft meditation today. All well... There is always noon tomorrow.

* * *

At noon today I embarked on my walk through the forest en route to the good doctor. I couldn't wait to hear what he had to say after having missed him yesterday for a very important meeting.

So it was with great purpose I hiked through the woods waving at my friend in the Hobbit House, grateful she didn't invite me in. I was already lining up the excuses should she call my name, but being the observant friend and neighbour I am sure she noticed my determined pace.

The courtesies of the city, hard habits to ignore, I knocked at the door of the cabin, but I was met with silence.

Although the door appeared ajar, it was with the hip that it dislodged and I tumbled in. With a sigh of relief I took note of the cabin checking that all was in its place, my eyes seeking out *The Doctor.*

"What wisdoms have you for me today?" I asked as I got comfortable on the futon.

> "I always have hopes of a man when I hear him confessing his sins," the doctor said cheerfully, "it's the man who confesses other men's sins that I cannot thole." (11)

How the doctor knew that I came here to write the sins of my parents, of my partner, of me I do not know. Maybe it was something I confessed to him two days ago, I was just so lost in myself I don't remember. I honestly thought confession good for the soul and a necessary means to happiness.

> "... Today is my 78th birthday—so you can take a word of advice from me," he continued, "never mind finding fault with the rest of the world, just try to make your own corner of it as happy as you can." (15)

I'm trying, good doctor. I'm trying to follow your model of the peace you bring to the visits and contacts you have with others. In your wake you always leave a current of hope, a transformation of pain to peace. But it's not easy. And for all the peace and harmony you bring to those you meet, you still feel the loneliness of the blanket of darkness.

Avoiding that blanket myself, I watch the flying ant pace the window, up the pane, fly away, fly into the window—smack, pace, smack, pace, smack—trying to find its way to the other side.

> Did anyone know good doctor that at the end of the day "with the shades of night a sense of [your] own loneliness oppressed [you]?" (16) Did you ever let anyone know that "the death of a summer day was always depressing" (28) to you? That night dreams of coffins and the "outward trappings of death" (29) wanted you? That you would sit by your fireside whispering like a tired child, "father take me home soon." (16)

* * *

At noon today with a heavy heart and heavy smell of forest repellant, I set off on my travels. Today is the last day I get to visit my good doctor. Although I am hoping he guides me to how this story ends, I am afraid.

My first visit is with my good friend John over on Long Island Pond. Many a night have John and I sat contemplating the mysteries of the Word over a bottle of scotch. Now John is a man so giving in nature that no one recognizes his gift of presence. So solid an ear he always gives, that he surprised me one night with talk of his anger at his words and giving up committing them to the page.

> "The voices," he said, "they just keep telling me that this is shit! What am I doing here? You can't do this."

> To which I replied, "Tell the voices to fuck off John! Just give them the finger and write anyway," and he smiled and nodded and we proceeded with Dun Bheagan.

Today however it was my turn to confess my fear to him trying to stretch my journey home. "I thought about my fear last night in the hazy darkness of Dun Bheagan. I came here in search of the validations of my story and I have found them. Now I have no excuse. The only person left in my way is me."

> "Yes," he said, "it is so much easier to fall back on not being able to do it, than to face doing it."
>
> "Good luck, my friend."
>
> "And to you," and with that I left his company and returned to the buzz of the forest around my ears.

As I approached my friend in the Hobbit House I reminisced the feelings of walking by with excitement to see you good doctor, but today I found my excuse to stop and chat and see how she was doing. It had been a few days since I'd visited the house and wanted to capture the moment on camera. Really I was just delaying my visit with you, good doctor.

"Denial is a great thing," our mentor said. "People don't recognize themselves in words, especially if the words coined them negatively." A sage piece of advice that you probably had a hand in imparting good doctor, one that I'm sure will come in handy as my pen will one day glide confessingly across the page.

Anita, my Hobbit House friend, need not worry about the published word for hers are already bought. Her solid advice and contribution to our mentor's experience were much appreciated and I look forward to reading her *Moose*.

I knocked.

"Come in. Close the door! Aren't they bad?!"

The bugs, I nodded, preoccupied with thoughts of seeing you. "I just stopped by to see how you were liking your place. It's very cool."

"Yes. It must be the rock. How is yours?"

"Fine once you get the windows open."

After a few quick pictures and mindful of the time and task at hand, I smiled and took my leave.

"Good writing!" Anita wished me. Yes good writing I thought, I hope, I pray as I slowed my pace to you good doctor pondering your parting words: "Father take me home soon."

* * *

At noon tonight my sleep disturbed by the nightmare of my seven-year-old daughter in the water, caught by a buck, and me yelling to move away as it kicked her beautiful self over and over. That horrible feeling of guilty helplessness replays every time I drift to dream so I think of Sheryl with an 'S' and you good doctor and the story you told at noon yesterday of a man who finally faced the grief of the death of his son some six years ago and you said, "there is something awesome in the grief of a strong man" or a strong woman, which is precisely how I feel in Sheryl's presence. Her calm courage blanketed me this night in my fear of sleep.

Wrapped in my blanket of courage, I stared out to the darkened sky and I heard the call of the loon. I smiled, another layer of peace enveloping me as I recalled Betty-Anne's impressions of me and comparing me to the loon, "You're just like the loon," she said, "trying to leave the water and take flight; but like the loon, you're never really sure if you're going to get off the water or not." I couldn't believe that was how people saw me, a light trying to fly. A loon, symbolic of "lucid dreaming and re-awakening of old hopes, wishes and dreams," I remembered reading in *Animal Speak* by Ted Andrews. Me. And the irony is that I am here trying to overcome the demons of my past and commit them to the page in the hopes of changing the consciousness of a planet.

> Like you did good doctor in your life because you "always brought out the best in everyone." (65) You were a man "of widest sympathy and most generous disposition...too big souled to descend to petty jealousy and [your] spirit loved to dwell on heaven and on life there."(67)

Thank you good doctor for leaving a trail of clues to your stories and thank you Ms. Isabel Cameron for committing the doctor's story to the page for me to find. That very action, capturing the doctor's essence in a "wee book" gave people peace then and now.

> "You remember the first time *The Doctor* was published?" Donald asked you Isabel, "My folks sent me a copy in the Christmas parcel, and I lent it to Sandy who lent it to another Morayshire 'loon.' Indeed *The Doctor* went up and down the line [the trenches] all that week." (74)

Pile of Rocks

by Amanda O'Donovan

I make my way down to the meadow, leaving behind the competitive screech of family voices, each seeking attention, voicing opinion, eager to take the stage, but never willing to listen for a response—pausing only for applause.

For a while, at least, they'll feed off each other, devouring the hubris that's in such plentiful supply.

Thoughts of Leonard Cohen swim from nowhere into my unguarded mind. Multiple versions of his exhausted anthem compete for my attention until KD Lang ties me to a kitchen chair, and the hallelujah chorus fades, allowing the optimism of the birdsong to take over.

I cross the corner of the meadow and reach my beloved rocks. What begins as a careless pile, related only by an uninspiring shade of grey, and perhaps a loose association of size and shape, quickly becomes the suggestion of a wall—a thread that ties the adobe building to the cool promise of the pond in the distance.

The rocks feel intensely familiar in a way that the family I've left behind is not. I even know the lichen that grows there. The vibrant greens, retaining all the plump promises of spring. The rusty splashes, as if spilt accidentally. The hopelessly crusty, black dehydrated scabs—and my favourite: the lichen whose ambitious, frilly edges suggest a flamboyance, an underwater connection and a determination to overcome an allotment of muted sage.

It's a place I come to mourn my losses and speak to my dead.

Hidden from the house, and generously shaded by two trees, whose names I do not know, these rocks accept me for who I am. The sunlight struggles to infiltrate this welcome patch of shade, fighting with the leafy canopy overhead to make its imprint and animate the surface of the rocks. The leaves that fill the voids between my rocks are enough to encourage determined dog roses to take root in the emptiness, adding a hopeful splash of colour. Rejected branches have fallen unwitnessed — sun-bleached, brittle and untidy.

I've exchanged the stifling proximity of family for the gentle winds that liberate my pile of rocks. Caught in the ambush of a merciless Ontario heatwave, the breezes counter with movement and sound. The song of sand in the dry hollow of bamboo. The whisper of Paddy Nolan, who never knew of the joy his lake would bring.

The displacement of air reveals a whole collection of meadow grasses, clamouring for my attention. The mini bulrushes that may be important enough to have a Latin name. The oat grasses with their stylish cloches and the feathery heads of grasses that have already gone to seed.

While the austerity of the rocks has drained colour and energy from its neighbouring flowers — stripping them of their vibrant purpose — the centre of the meadow reveals the reds, purples, pinks and blues of vetch, clover and ripening berries, the innocent upturned faces of daisies and the obediently nodding stands of milk weed.

The screen of trees on the far side of the gravel drive marks the edge of the world I have momentarily misplaced. They are unapologetically and emeraldly green against the two-dimensional disappointment of a perfectly blue sky.

In another life, at another moment, things would have been different.

I am temporarily distracted by the dance of two undistinguished butterflies, marking out the playful ritual of children who know they must release their fanciful energy before someone older intervenes. I catch sight of the lone sumac in the centre of the meadow. Bent by the wind, the ailing tree points me in the direction of the house, comically refusing to acknowledge its accelerating baldness — resolutely clinging to its four remaining tufts of leaves.

The bitching insistence of the deer flies takes me back to a place that I know. The community of family has the power to build or destroy.

As I leave the meadow, I notice a single splash of orange among the blues, pinks and purples. Why here? Why now? I take a deep breath and let the singular burnt orange petals remind me that there's nothing wrong with being different.

My Chosen Place

by Audrey Ogilvie

The veranda at Wintergreen is my vantage point. My temporary hide-out. My look-out on the world. I wondered if it was laziness that made me choose the closest writing place, the one closest to the kitchen and the emergency chocolate. No, it wasn't. I am naturally attracted to colour, texture, and variety. This spot has it all.

The tongue and groove ceiling catches my eye. I know I will be able to come back here some day and see the patina it will develop. The vertical support beams have already nicely weathered, thanks to their exposure to the elements. Sturdy textured tiles cover the decking, reminiscent of dwellings in other parts of the world. The neatly piled logs must come from the acreage that's large enough to sustain winter warmth, possibly forever.

The visible semi-circle of majestic trees is evident, even through closed eyes. It's as if they are gossiping—passing along information that is important to know. They exude life and kind of tender heartedness, right to the tips of their branches. The scale of most trees puts us in our place while at the same time making us feel we are somehow insulated from harm. There is something tranquilizing about their presence. They help being alone feel comfortable.

Songbirds hide in the leaves but make their presence known. A queen bee swoops as if she's simply taking a break from the routine of her life. Her sound is one of so many sounds, but there is no cacophony in nature. The clouds have wispy edges and in places the soft white diminishes to a pale mouse grey. One looks as if it has a soft underbelly of moisture but it's quickly being nudged by the wind to a place outside of my field of vision.

The breeze freshens and the ornamental grasses that border the gravel walkway do their own swaying hula.

Today Monet has painted the sky.

I am facing an outer corner of the veranda, watching hollyhocks bobbing backwards and forwards. They look like whimsical sentinels towering over the low-slung plants beneath them. I can see the green remnants of peonies and irises that on the other side of the walkway morph into ornamental grasses, brilliant peach and red lilies joined by purple and white Echinacea. In their own circle, nubby daisy heads sway to and fro as if to say, "We're next." Those hollyhocks remind me of lazy afternoons in Toronto many years ago.

There is something both supreme and serene in this snapshot of rural Ontario. Two lovingly crafted small buildings with flat sod roofs have risen out of the earth and are also a part of it. They look so at home here. Each has a clearly defined function.

A black urn stands solidly, anchoring the end of the veranda that serves as an entrance to the main building. It holds fuchsia, impatiens and some trailing white lobelia. A momentary nod to formality.

I have always fancied building a rock wall and think about that possibility as I look at one that divides the meadow from the winding flagstone pathway. As I look to my extreme right there is a patch of orange day lilies, those stalwart native plants that can always be counted on to bloom, no matter how harsh a winter and spring has been.

It's so beautiful here. I can't help but think of the horror of being blind. I wonder if one had never seen anything if some hidden part of the imagination comes to life. A hummingbird has just motored inches from my head. I have never been close enough to hear the surprisingly loud noise those tiny wings are capable of making. Provencal blue and yellow flowers bloom below the Shasta daisies. I realise that where I am sitting — at a round metal table with lacy little chairs — I could be in France. Or, more precisely, in Provence. This world is more peppered with similarities than we know.

Today David Milne has painted the sky.

It has been raining off and on and the trees seem to have closed ranks. I know their semi-circle hasn't gotten smaller. It only feels that way. Despite the lack of sun, the flowers seem more vibrant than ever. Some daisy heads are poised to explode. The three buildings I can see amaze me. So solid and pretty, the grass on their sod roofs stands stalk still today.

Below the meadow is a duck pond. Quiet, reflective water. The duck pond looks like it's exactly where it should be. I know there is poison ivy lurking around on these 204 acres. Yesterday I was reminded of the expression, "Leaves of three, let it be." Butterflies are at home here. They waft on the wind and come close as if to reassure us that not all is wrong with this world. Allergies have made my head feel as if it is stuck in clay. That the top of my head is somewhere else. It feels removed, however, it seems to be responsible for the never-ending flow that blocks my ears and my nose. A nuisance.

The sun has broken through the steely ceiling. Laser beams at first and then klieg lights. The perfect set for something dramatic, romantic or simply routine.

A.Y. Jackson painted the sky with soft silver and then handed the brush to William Gainsborough.

The daisy heads have twisted to face the sun. They now look like botanical electric toothbrushes but by this time tomorrow they may be smiling. Today is still. There is barely a ripple through the leaves. The hummingbirds swing close again before doing a major dance and then diving down to sip the lilies. The duck pond is dark with a striated surface of taupe growth. I wonder what has encouraged that. Maybe rotting wood. It doesn't seem possible that anything toxic could have leached into the water. But that's only because I have no idea of its size — of its circumference. Any variety of things happen in unseen places.

The deerflies seem to have taken a holiday. Perhaps they don't like the lack of humidity. I do. It occurs to me to imagine myself in a wheelchair, condemned to this veranda. I would have about thirty feet to roll back and forth on. During the four seasons of the year there would necessarily be many changes. What lays behind the trees whose leaves fall in autumn? The crisp air would encourage battalions of birds to head south, their choreography better than Martha Graham's. I wonder if I would be aware of the crickets leaving. In fact, I wonder where they go. Do they hibernate, do they live in tunnels under the snow? Or do they simply die? On this veranda I would anticipate spring with an unparalleled eagerness. I suspect one could never be lonely here.

Today Jackson Pollack jessoed the sky and then turned over the brush to Emily Carr.

Dragonfly Writing

by Sophie Ogilvie-Hanson

In the living room of the house where I grew up, one of the grainy yellow walls was decorated with paintings, posters, any other trinket that matched. On it a fish hung from a nail that was sloppily hammered in at a ninety degree angle. I could pull it off the wall and shift its tail, vertebrae by vertebrae. Some of its scales shone like the core of a clam shell, transporting me back to barefooted afternoons spent combing the beaches of the Bay of Fundy for glass worn down by ocean salts. Others were covered in a pearly gloss like a sheet of undeveloped photographic paper. I would fit the fish in both palms and run it over my fingers, always tempted to try to break it in half, only because I knew that I couldn't. I remember admiring the sculpture of a dragonfly that laid next to the fish, made of bronze and blown glass. The sea foam blue wings were almost reminiscent of a St. Patrick's cathedral's stained-glass window panels.

The most interesting thing about dragonflies is their seemingly transparent wings. Wading through a lake of tall brown grasses, UV rays punishing me for my lack of sunscreen, I found myself compelled to take a seat and watch as what looked like two electric blue toothpicks flew by. One was on top of the other. As I studied I became increasingly aware of the golfball eyes that appeared to be staring back at me. There is a sense of anxiety that comes from the prying eyes of a stranger, that can't really exist artificially. I get this feeling sitting alone on the subway sometimes, or walking past the Portuguese dance club near my house at night. I can only imagine how zoo animals under constant scrutiny must feel. This is pretty hypocritical of me, actually. I have a tendency to stare at people that I find either very interesting or fascinatingly boring. I'm sure I cause people on the subway a bit of anxiety too. It's just strange that I feel the same amount of stress from a someone that could cause me psychical harm and something I could squish between two fingers.

As I engaged in my staring contest with my new-found component, an ant began to climb up my leg. Out of instinct I kicked it away with the opposite foot, ripping off its hind legs and sending it flying to the ground. I was dumbstruck with my ability to take away a life, as I had proven without a second thought. I'm not the type of person to imagine that ant with a family, a home, and ambitions. It's simply peculiar that because of me that life no longer exists. From then on I acted as a jungle gym for each ant, bee, wasp, and even dragonfly. I watched proudly as the bee flew away into the petals of an ivory flower, identical to the top of a phonograph, its only song being the mundane humming of its flapping wings.

Nomenclature of the Meadow Flowers

by Joyce Sheehey

A visit to the meadow reminds her
How much there is to be learned
Or perhaps confirms how poor a student she must have been.
For only a few of nature's names
Remain in her memory,
And the flypaper quality that attaches words to brain —
for her —
Well, flypaper holds only flies.

In Wintergreen's nearby meadowland, two
flowers she identifies with certainty:
The *Daisy* (which every toddler recognizes)
And the storied, romantic *Queen Anne's Lace*.
And the others?

As a child, the teaching she was privileged to
Held the code to unlock the meadow's nomenclature:
Nuns in habits and practical shoes, leading
children through the grounds.
Beyond the convent,
Kneeling, one with the earth,
Recited the names as they embraced the precious flora...
Red Clover, Goldenrod, Indian Paintbrush,
Yarrow, Joe Pye, and then, closer to the forest,
Jacob's Ladder, Jack-in-the-Pulpit.

Now, batting away persistent flies, she
discovers a new meadow,
Only to find she cannot call the flowers by their names.
And so she chooses to do God's bidding — to
name the plants of the earth
To demonstrate dominion,
Since names ascribed by others have long
ago died away.

The long stalks of tiny white flowers ascending
in dainty pattern becomes *Milkmaid's Footprints.*
The violet bunches of rounded petals, hanging
like grapes, she names *Banquo,*
For the honorable, unlucky friend of Macbeth.
The tall, upright tower with scores of leaves,
each smaller than the last, each like a step,
Leading to the tiny powder white pillow in its center
She chooses to call *Journey's Rest.*
The five-petaled soft yellow floweret sitting at meadow's edge
She names *Butterscotch Star,*
And picking a dozen of them on a summer's day
in a not so distant future
She will say to their lucky recipient, not, *Here
are some Butterscotch Stars for you,*
But rather, *I've brought you a constellation of Butterscotch.*
Finally, the tall stems of blue handbells she'll call
Lover's Secret –
The flower appeals, yet she who holds it soon learns
of the secret spike
At flower's center — advertising the hurt inside.
Lover's Secret feels most appropriate.

She dreams that she returns to the teachers
of her childhood,
And, climbing the convent hill, she carries a
bouquet of flowers —

A testament of gratitude —
Tied with a purple bow.

She has gathered her meadow flowers, and
those, too, newly baptized, *Payne's Propeller*,
Fleance (a lesser known variety of the
species *Banquo*),
As well as the large-bodied, conspicuous and
vulgar *Flagstaff's Belch*.

In case there's no one home, or the nuns
have died away,
She leaves a note with her bouquet:

To the Sisters of Mercy, my teachers —
here's belated thanks —
For all the things you taught me
That I thought I had forgotten.

The Behaviour of Turtles
by Nathalie Sorensen

In the shine of July afternoons, I sit watching the pond,
taking notes: blue sky, white puffs of cloud reflected,
smooth surface stippled in yellow water weeds.

Two turtles, wet backs glistening, clamber up a log,
bask two minutes, slip back into water. A breeze
riffles the surface, rustling leaves on young elms,
bending reeds, cooling my face. A warbler calls;
the turtles climb back on the log, walk, jump off.

A leopard frog croaks his two notes on my left, another
answers right. A dragonfly lands on my notebook,
spreads itself over my words, punctuates them with four
black dots on the tips of lacy wings. One turtle, then
another climbs on the log, then jumps off. A leopard frog
croaks, a choir of bullfrogs answer.

In the house above the pond,
a young woman roasts zucchini, Portobello mushrooms,
eggplant, over hot coals; her neighbour nurses her
newborn; beside her a philosopher ponders the problem
which will occupy the rest of her life.

The turtles climb a smaller log,
fall off, swim over to the larger, climb on, jump down
into a round white cloud. The baby falls asleep, bullfrogs
croak, a breeze dances the reeds, the cook makes
strawberry trifle, the philosopher reads Merleau-Ponty.

The dragonfly and
I make another note in the glow of this pond afternoon.

Observations and Reflections from Wintergreen

by Cheryl Sutherland

Monday, July 9

I sit atop a large rock. More like a boulder really. I am surrounded by forest and the laneway into Wintergreen is a stone's throw away. I have let this place find me as I walked away from the main Wintergreen building in search of my spot. Initially, I walked on past the rock; perhaps anticipating that there would be a better place for me further along. But the image of the rock nestled within the trees would not let go of its hold on me and so I have returned to the place that already felt somehow familiar. As though the place had already claimed me.

On my way to this spot I saw a wild turkey dancing through the trees, the crackling of dead leaves from last autumn announcing her presence. The sound of her leaving was a hastily paced rustling and pattering through the foliage. The sound becoming less and less as she moved away from me.

It is nearing mid-afternoon and the sun is high in the sky. There are spotlights of light filtering down through the tree tops. A slight breeze is singing ... robins are chirping ... a loud squirrel pontificates from somewhere in the forest.

Staring down from my perch on the rock I can see the blanketing layers of dead leaves, similar to those the turkey was dancing through earlier. Amidst the decaying leaves there are tiny trees that have broken through the leaf blanket. Saplings. Death and rebirth entwined. The leaves providing part of the foundation that allow the saplings to grow and survive. Each one playing its role in the circle of life. Each one making its distinct mark on the landscape.

The shape of the rock I am sitting on is difficult to describe. It is not round, but roundish. It is not square, but does have some sides that are straight-edged. It is definitely not very comfortable for sitting on, but I make the best of it.

On the northwest side of the rock is an elaborate spider web. How appropriate I think to myself. The spider represents creativity and connection and the spider has recently become one of my totems.

The first time I visited Wintergreen, my first non-human encounter was with a rather large, furry garden spider who scurried quickly across my path. I took the sighting as a good sign, as though she were saying: "This is the place to come and be creative."

I am relieved, however, that the spider to my side now is small, thin, and not at all furry in appearance.

Tuesday, July 10

I have arrived to my perch on the rock earlier today than yesterday. The sun is still being filtered by the leaves, not yet having reached the opening that will allow it to beat down fully upon me.

The robins chirp from somewhere in the trees on the other side of the laneway. The breeze from yesterday is currently absent, as is the spider. Although her web is still intact.

The deer flies have yet to find me, but a few pesky mosquitoes are humming their annoying tune around my ears. The occasional dragonfly drifts past, as if simply out of curiosity. Wondering why I am here.

Later. A chipmunk has just ventured towards me. A throaty warning clucking from her mouth. She looks as though she is making some kind of announcement. As though she is asking: "What the hell is that? And why is whatever that is sitting there…it must be lost."

The chipmunk edges slowly closer, eyes blinking rather dramatically and her tail pointed straight in the air, like an antenna. Staring and then deciding it is too risky, or too undesirable, to come any closer. Suddenly, she turns and with a quick flick of her tail, scampers off in the opposite direction and disappears.

My place quiets again.

Later. As much as I try, my mind cannot help going there. I try to force the story to wait until later, but the thought of this time last year is too strong. It will not go away.

This time last year, Daniela was released from Kingston General Hospital after being hospitalized for six days. I have photographs of her taken on this day last year. The two of us on our deck, our faces beaming at the reality of being home together. Our hopes for a life together were forefront in our minds. Our future still an open book, filled with possibilities and opportunities to live happily ever after.

The earth-shattering diagnosis was still three days away.

Why did so many things in Daniela's life in Canada happen in threes?

She lived in three different towns. She held three different jobs. She obtained three different degrees. She had three different kinds of cancer. She lived for three months and three days after being diagnosed.

With grief, time becomes suspended. The past and the present jumble together. The memories put into some kind of memory-mixer, thrown together, shaken furiously, and then let loose. As though upon release, everything is supposed to come together again in some kind of coherent framework. As if it is all somehow supposed to make some kind of sense. I am still trying to figure it out.

Back to the present.

The birds seem to have moved in closer. I can now see them flying from branch to branch on the other side of the laneway. The breeze is more evident. The feeling, the heaviness of the emotion is lifting.

I have come to believe that the act of writing is a passage to healing and understanding. A means of beginning to integrate everything—the emotions, the memories, the trauma. Writing is a means of reconciling the loss and slowly inching forward.

Wednesday July 11

The sun today is positioned in the open spot in the trees. My rock is directly in the path of the sun and it is hot.

The spider's web is still in place, but the spider itself is again absent. The birds continue to sing as though they never stop. Ever. The chipmunk from yesterday is nowhere in sight.

I feel a certain sense of excitement today, as though I am on the edge of something new. A new beginning, a new adventure, a new direction.

We walked down to the lake after lunch today. Sitting on the dock, gazing out across the lake, I suddenly spotted a deer on the other side. Gentleness and innocence; a gentle luring to new adventure … one reading of the deer as a totem.

I have seen deer every day during my time at Wintergreen. It is difficult for me to ignore the significance. Nor do I want to. I do not want to ignore how powerful and transformative this moment in my life is. I do not want to let go of the creative direction that my life is taking. I do not want to try and fit myself back into a mold in which I know I no longer fit.

Everything has changed.

There is no going back, there is only moving ahead. Like a character in a story: what is it that I want to happen? What kind of re-storying of my life do I want to take place? What are the pieces of the jigsaw puzzle that might fit back together? What are the pieces that are gone forever? What are the new pieces I can create?

Perhaps living life is like writing a story where the only thing you know for sure, or think that you know, is the part that has already taken place. You can try to create the conditions by which you fabricate a new life, but even then all you can do is to try and make choices in the moment, based on the knowledge you have, and hope that is all turns out okay.

I heard a line from a movie recently where the character says: "Everything will be alright in the end, and so if it is not yet alright, then it is not yet the end."

I find this thought comforting. Especially in the midst of chaos. It is comforting to think that everything will be alright in the end.

Thursday , July 12

It is warmer today. There is a breeze. The soft rustling of blowing leaves near the tops of the trees and a crow cawing in the distance are the predominant sounds of the moment.

The spider web seems to have disappeared overnight. Vanished. I hope this is not indicative of my own creativity.

Joyce is approaching, on towards her place in the meadow. We compare deer fly reports as she ventures past.

Today is the last day of observation and I have to admit that I already feel as though I am going to miss it. It has been refreshing to have the opportunity to be part of a group; a group with similar aspirations. It has been a valuable experience to engage in this type of observation. A reminder that when you slow down and allow yourself to be more in tune with your surroundings, you create a place of peace within yourself.

Peace seems hard to come by these days. What are the ingredients to obtaining a peaceful state of mind? Is it having purpose? Feeling loved? Having financial security and good health? Is it the absence of pain?

This time last year, this very day, was the day before Daniela's death sentence diagnosis. It was our last day of trying to hold our worst fears at bay. Our last day of ignoring the ever-present, just-below-the-surface, bubbling anxiety.

I remember it as a good day. This time last year. The day was beautiful and sunny, like today. Daniela and I talked, we laughed, we lived in the moment. We did not waste our time worrying about what was yet to come.

Long Pond Island: A Song in Three Parts

by David White

Each day after lunch I made my way down the main trail across the bridge and onto the rock overlooking Long Pond Island. As I settled in, first Helen and Charlotte and then Christine and Cynthia walked by smiling encouragement as my time of writing began. I came to Wintergreen with two stories begging for my attention; Joe Indian and the story of Bill and Orv. As I sat on my rock, the following reflections emerged.

Long Pond Island: Part 1

The wind was fresh, drying the dirt and sweat of the foundry, the blood pooling on my white-ribbed T-shirt as I sat on the rock at the edge of "The Pot," the Pottawatami River. The horn of a freighter leaving the Harbour drifted in on the edge of the breeze, bringing her words back to me… "Coward" she spat, as she pushed back from her embrace, sticking me with the white feather, the blood oozing from the prick, as her black hair flicked across my face like the slap of a horse's tail, her nipple poking through the thin fabric of her blouse. A coward, because I was not in uniform, like Orv and his crowd, Tommy and Red and so many others from my town. A coward, because I was not yet 16 and had not lied about my age. Not yet 16, but working at the Foundry, usually the night shift…the whine of the lathes still ringing in my ears, the metal filings clinging to the soles of my boots, to the cuff of my pants, the grease oozing from my pores.

A frog hops off the lily pad, rippling into the cool stream, it was just around the next bend where Orv and I used to fish and just around the next bend after that where we used to spy on the Turner girls skinny-dipping, their long blonde curls plastered against their wet skin, Orv leaning around the Maple to get a better look,… only to lean too far, his splash louder than any frog falling off a lily pad, the girls screaming and thrashing out of the river, scrambling up the bank, laughing and pretending to be angry as they ran off.

"Coward." Her words continued to sting as I peeled off my clothes and with them the blood, sweat and dirt and dived in, the call of the freighter haunting and beckoning me to swim out further from shore and away… or was it back?

Long Pond Island: Part 2

I don't remember…I don't remember the name my Grandmother gave me. It had been whispered to her in the song of the pines, in the breakfast jack-hammering of the woodpecker, in the twitch of the cricket in evening. She had told it to me in the warmth of her back as we kneeled to the meadow, her fingers stained with the juice of the strawberries and blueberries found in the beginnings of the new forest.

I lost that name in the slap of your school teachers as I spoke my language, in your Churches filled with sacrifice and blood, staining my soul… in the steel and concrete of your cities.

I have not found it in the concrete and steel of your cities…I have not found it in the whiskey and smoke…I have not found it in the rage of my fists…in the cuts and bruises of the street, embedded in my knuckles.

I hear the whisper of the Maple, the call of the Jack… I watch the ripple of the deer fly landing in the pond…the sun drenches and drips and then I hear the circling bush planes, descending, and gathering and returning to the unquenchable fires and the voices of the priests, the teachers return, drowning out the whispers of the Grandmothers.

"Joe." "Joe Indian." That's your name—that's who you are—broken, savage, in need of redemption … I don't remember.

Long Pond Island: Part 3

I have found my rock, covered in lichen, bits of moss. Scrub trees— maples, elms, vines—green and red, dried long grass pops up here and there. The breeze whispers, consoles and urges me to write, speaks my name and reminds me who I was created to be. A deer fly swarms and distracts and disappears, only to appear once again. Dead trees emerge from the pond—smooth and weathered—or are they dead? Leaning, twisted and gnarled sentries—like old folks sitting in wheel chairs at the entrance of the Nursing Home, hollowed out from the years, from the many seasons of their lives—what wonders lie within, what knowledge, what wisdom, what storms have arisen, what heat and cold, rain and snow. Perfect blue, wisps of cloud, of heat shimmering like a mirage in the desert, holding the promise of change and beginnings, lily pads interrupting the shadows and reflections of the trees, rocks, insects and sky.

In my city, I yearn for this quiet, this peace, away from e-mail and cell phones, from the poverty and loss, away from the anxiety of those desperately hanging on to the last years of a dying institution, an institution that seems no longer relevant, whose voice seems unable to proclaim hope, welcome and inclusion. An institution, that too often offers only judgement and restriction, rather than welcome and freedom.

The breeze quickens, cleanses and makes new and the world is calm but not quiet, crickets twitch and birds send out their warning, or is it a beckoning to come closer…a leaf plops into the pond and ripples and ripples until it is still. But stillness is an illusion in this place, there is a hum of busyness that I am barely glimpsing. I am the centre of my universe, but not of this universe, this universe that stirs and thrives despite me and what it is that I notice. Communication surrounds me, if I only have the heart and the ears to listen.

A pilliated woodpecker, its brilliant red head, sails off in search of fresh food. I watch as two leaves flutter to the pond, actually, one leaf flutters and the other drops like a stone. A dragonfly is perched on the tree sticking out of the pond, teal the colour of the wings. Long Pond Island.

The Writers

Jennifer Bennett is a gardener, writer, and musician. Jennifer has written many books on gardening, including *The New Northern Gardener*, *Dryland Gardening: Plants That Survive and Thrive in Tough Conditions*, and *Lilies of the Hearth: The Historical Relationship between Women and Plants*. Jennifer lives not far from Wintergreen.

Sandra Brooks lives in Kingston, Ontario with her partner Deb, three cats and a sizable spider that lives behind the driver side mirror of their car. This is her first appearance in a publication that might actually be read by other people and this tickles her to no end. She hopes someday to see more of her work in print but knows that making that hope come to fruition will require corralling the feral gaggle of ideas currently roaming wild and free in her office.

Helen Coo lives in Kingston, Ontario. Her piece, "My Mom's Love Affair with Campbells," appeared in the Facts and Arguments column of *The Globe & Mail*. Helen is a well-loved volunteer in the Wintergreen kitchen.

Mary Corkery has worked many decades for social justice, the past eight years with KAIROS: Canadian Ecumenical Justice Initiatives. She has now retired and gives proper attention to her jealous writing. Her poems have been published in *The Whetstone*, *The New Quarterly*, and *Our Times Magazine*, and several will appear in an upcoming issue of the *The Antigonish Review*.

Diana Claire Douglas is an artist, writer, educator, and Systemic Constellation Work facilitator. Following her creative spirit where it wishes to take her has meant her life has been quite the adventure! She presently resides in Ottawa, Ontario.

Christine Fischer Guy's short fiction has appeared in *Descant, Prairie Fire*, and *Grimm* and has been nominated for the Journey Prize. Her first novel, *Moose*, debuts in 2014. She reviews fiction for *The Globe and Mail* and has conducted podcasts for Bookninja.com. She has lived and worked in London, England and now makes her home in Toronto. Her website is christinefischerguy.com.

Elizabeth Greene has published two books of poetry, *The Iron Shoes* (Hidden Brook, 2007) and *Moving* (Inanna, 2010). Her work has appeared in the *Literary Review of Canada*, *The Antigonish Review, freefall,* and the *Queen's Feminist Review* and in several anthologies, most recently *Poet to Poet Anthology* (Guernica, 2012, ed. Elana Wolff and Julie Roorda). She edited and contributed to *We Who Can Fly: Poems, Essays and Memories in Honour of Adele Wiseman,* which won the Betty and Morris Aaron Prize for Best Scholarship on a Canadian Subject in 1998. She lives in Kingston with her son and three cats.

Karen Holmes is a spiritual director, storyteller and remedial teacher who lives on a biodynamic garden/orchard in Bellrock ON with her partner, Kevin, several chickens, a dog and their Russian bees.

Betty-Anne Howard is a Financial Planner with a social conscience who truly believes in making dreams a reality, including her own. She runs her own business, grew up poor and stopped feeling sorry for herself a long time ago. For her, creativity is the answer to most things, that and having fun.

Lorrie Jorgensen is a tradeswoman who started her working career as a secretary in 1977. Quickly finding out it wasn't for her, she moved into the auto body repair and refinishing trade as an apprentice. Once licensed she worked for the City of Ottawa and then went on to teach her trade, plus welding and introduction to motor vehicle programs for Women in Trades & Technology at Algonquin College. In 2003 she graduated from Queen's Technological Education Program and started on the insane and chaotic, yet extremely gratifying task of teaching tech in a high school. Lorrie has been published twice by *The Globe and Mail* and lives in Eastern Ontario with 4 dogs, 1 cat, and a wife.

Danny Lalonde is a writer and an educator. He lives near Kingston, Ontario. Harvest was written at Wintergreen Studios and published by *Queen's Quarterly* in 2011.

Ellen McKeough is a physician who practices in the many jails and prisons in the Kingston area. She has published short stories in several anthologies, including *Coming Attractions 91*. She attended Helen Humphreys' 2011 workshop, where she enjoyed the food, the lake, the writing instruction, and gleaned an outline for a novel from the group's *ad hoc* discussions about plot development. Ellen is currently at work on her third (unpublished) novel.

Lindy Mechefske is a freelance writer, editor, and photographer, and associate editor of the *Queen's Alumni Review*. She has lived in England, the USA, and Australia, and currently makes her home in Kingston, Ontario. She has a background in environmental science, a passion for rugged outdoor activities, and a lifelong love affair with food and cooking. Her cookbook, *A Taste of Wintergreen,* came about as a result of volunteering in the kitchen at Wintergreen Studios. Lindy's recent work has appeared in *The Ottawa Citizen, Montreal Gazette, Vancouver Sun, Kingston-Whig Standard, Kingston Life, Kingston Life Interiors,* and the *Queen's Feminist Review*. She is hard at work on a couple of book-length manuscripts that she hopes might actually make it past the slush pile somewhere one day. You can find her blogging about life in the kitchen at www.lindymechefske.com.

Cynthia Mitchell is a single mother of two beautiful daughters. She is a writer and a mystic. She is passionate about changing the consciousness of a planet. And during the day she is a secondary school English teacher.

Living and working in Europe and North America, **Amanda O'Donovan's** blend of business communication, marketing and operational experience reflects her ability to think beyond boundaries. She started her career with Unilever, in sales, marketing and operational roles in both the UK and Belgium. Amanda has since worked as an independent communications specialist for international corporations, entrepreneurs and non-profits across a wide cross-section of markets. Amanda lives in Unionville with her husband Sean, and has two twenty-something daughters, Hannah and Rebecca.

Audrey Ogilvie recorded a spoken word CD, *Canary*, in 2003 and in 2008 Waterfront Books, Burlington, VT, published a chapbook, *Enough White Lies to Ice a Cake*. Her work has also been published in *freefall*, a Detroit publication, *nth position*, UK, an anthology, *Poems from the Feminist Caucus, League of Canadian Poets, Frank Magazine* and numerous other periodicals. She has written two full-length novels that will be published shortly.

Sophie Ogilvie-Hanson lives, writes, and sings in Toronto, Ontario.

Joyce Sheehey has been teaching English for twenty years, from the high desert of New Mexico to Vermont's Green Mountains. Currently she teaches high school students in a suburb of Burlington, Vermont. She is spending the 2012–2013 school year on a leave of absence, in the quiet, rustic beauty of Sherkin Island, Ireland.

Nathalie Sorensen has been writing poetry for most of the last decade after a lifetime of reading it. She taught English at St. Lawrence College and studied English literature and education. She lives in Kingston and enjoys gardening, taking photographs and spending time with her family at their weekend house on the Salmon River.

Cheryl Sutherland is currently working on her first novel and studies human geography at Queen's University. She lives on a small acreage north of Kingston, which she shares with her two dogs, Chinook and Pepper.

David White lives in Cantley, Quebec with his partner Janine and their wonderful dog Einstein. He loves to write, listen to jazz, and enjoys a good single malt.

Wintergreen Studios Press is an independent literary press. It is affiliated with the not-for-profit educational retreat centre, Wintergreen Studios, and supports the work of Wintergreen Studios by publishing works related to education, the arts, and the environment.

www.wintergreenstudiospress.com
www.wintergreenstudios.com

Made in the USA
Charleston, SC
26 November 2012